Edward Graham Daves

Maryland and North Carolina in the Campaign of 1780-1781

Edward Graham Daves

Maryland and North Carolina in the Campaign of 1780-1781

ISBN/EAN: 9783337811693

Printed in Europe, USA, Canada, Australia, Japan

Cover: Foto ©ninafisch / pixelio.de

More available books at **www.hansebooks.com**

Fund-Publication, No. 33.

Maryland and North Carolina in the Campaign of 1780=1781:

WITH A PRELIMINARY NOTICE OF THE
EARLIER BATTLES OF THE REVOLUTION, IN WHICH THE TROOPS
OF THE TWO STATES WON DISTINCTION.

A Paper read before the Maryland Historical Society,

November 14th, 1892,

By EDWARD GRAHAM DAVES,

A MEMBER OF THE SOCIETY.

Baltimore, 1893.

Maryland and North Carolina in the Campaign of 1780-1781.

Monument to the Maryland Line on Guilford Battle-Field, Dedicated 15 October, 1892.

Fund-Publication, No. 33.

Maryland and North Carolina in the Campaign of 1780=1781:

WITH A PRELIMINARY NOTICE OF THE
EARLIER BATTLES OF THE REVOLUTION, IN WHICH THE TROOPS
OF THE TWO STATES WON DISTINCTION.

A Paper read before the Maryland Historical Society,

November 14th, 1892,

By EDWARD GRAHAM DAVES,

A MEMBER OF THE SOCIETY.

Baltimore, 1893.

PEABODY PUBLICATION FUND.

COMMITTEE ON PUBLICATION.

1892-93.

HENRY STOCKBRIDGE,
BRADLEY T. JOHNSON,
CLAYTON C. HALL.

The Committee on Publication desire it to be understood that neither they, nor the Society, assume any responsibility for the statements or opinions expressed by the authors of the Publications issued under their supervision.

PRINTED BY JOHN MURPHY & CO.
PRINTERS TO THE MARYLAND HISTORICAL SOCIETY.
BALTIMORE, 1893.

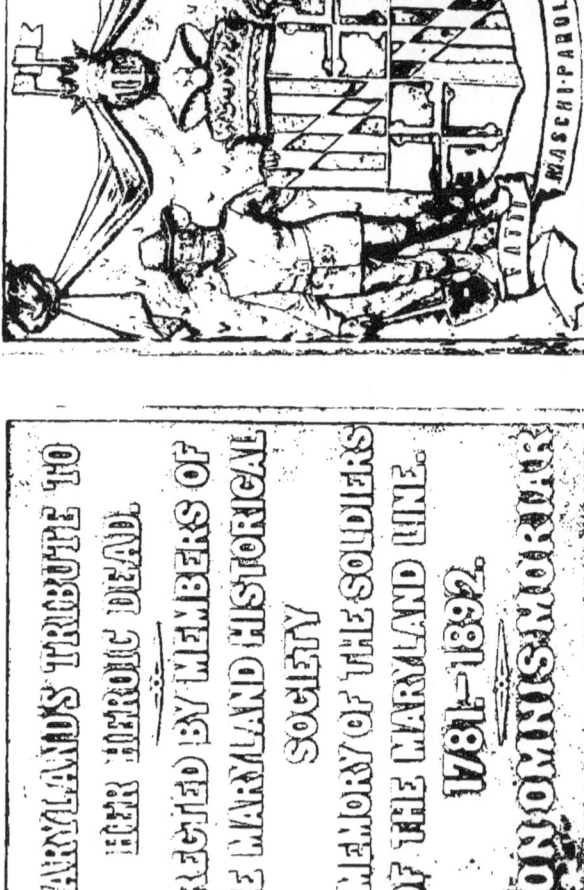

Bronze Tablets of the Maryland Monument.

GUILFORD BATTLE-MONUMENT.

By an Act of the Legislature of North Carolina of March 7th, 1887, a Charter of incorporation was granted to the Guilford Battle-Ground Company, an association formed for the "purpose of preserving and adorning the grounds on which the battle of Guilford Court House was fought on March 15th, 1781, and for the erection thereon of monuments to commemorate the heroic deeds of the American patriots who participated in this battle for liberty and independence." Organizing under this Charter, the Company bought a tract of seventy-five acres, including all the points of historic interest on the field; this has been cleared of undergrowth, and converted into a beautiful park. The grounds are fortunately almost untouched by the hand of time; the primitive forest is still there, the natural features of the spot are quite unchanged, and all the positions of the troops are readily recognizable.

As the soldiers of the Maryland Line played so conspicuous a part at the battle of Guilford, it seemed most fitting that their heroism should be commemorated by a suitable memorial. At a meeting of the Maryland Historical Society on June 8th, 1891, a committee consisting of Edward Graham Daves, Bradley T. Johnson, and W. Hall Harris, was appointed to take the matter into consideration. On November

9th they made a report, earnestly recommending the erection of a Maryland monument on the battle-field, and suggesting that the funds required for that purpose be raised by voluntary subscription among the members of the Society. The committee was instructed to carry into effect this recommendation: the plans were soon matured and carried out; the monument was unveiled with formal ceremonies on October 15th, 1892, and entrusted to the keeping of the Guilford Battle-Ground Company.

It is a rough block of Maryland granite, about five feet cube, raised upon a sodded base to the height of seven feet. Two of its faces are adorned with bronze tablets measuring 18 by 21 inches; one containing the arms of Maryland, the other the inscription of dedication:

MARYLAND'S TRIBUTE TO
HER HEROIC DEAD.
ERECTED BY MEMBERS OF
THE MARYLAND HISTORICAL
SOCIETY,
IN MEMORY OF THE SOLDIERS
OF THE MARYLAND LINE.
1781–1892.
NON OMNIS MORIAR.

The site is a commanding one, overlooking the whole of that portion of the field which was the scene of the gallant conduct of the Maryland troops.

The following paper is substantially the same as the address of dedication, which was delivered on the battle-ground at the unveiling of the monument. Numerous quotations are embodied in the text, the purpose being to let the actors in the drama and their contemporaries tell their own story; though, to economize space, many of the citations have been condensed.

Acknowledgments are due to Major Graham Daves of New Bern, and J. S. Bassett, Esq. of Durham, N. C., for valuable assistance in collecting historical data.

BALTIMORE, *January*, 1893.

MARYLAND AND NORTH CAROLINA IN THE CAMPAIGN OF 1780-1781.

THE erection of a monument by members of the Maryland Historical Society, on the battle-field of Guilford in North Carolina, in memory of the valour of Maryland soldiers, recalls to mind the many events of the Revolution in which the two States were brought together in helpful friendship or generous emulation. Each has won special distinction; both may be proud of their interesting and honourable record.

North Carolina was the mother of the Colonies, and within her borders was born the first white American. Her Regulators offered the first armed resistance to British authority, and at Alamance, in 1771, was shed the first blood in the struggle for liberty. At Mecklenburg, on 20th May, 1775, was made the first Declaration of Independence; and when hostilities had begun, North Carolina was the first Colony to vote explicitly for absolute separation from the mother country.[1] The brilliant victory of the patriots at Moore's Creek, on 27th February, 1776, prevented the junction of the British troops and the Scotch Loyalists, and foiled the purposed invasion of the Province by Sir Henry Clinton.[2] When the Provincial Congress at Halifax, on 12th April, 1776, instructed the North Carolina Delegates to the Continental Congress to vote for the independence of all the Colonies, one-third of her adults were already in the field.

Maryland, on the other hand, was the parent of religious toleration, which is the foundation stone of Colonial liberty. She first took practical steps towards severing her connection with the crown, and her delegates were the first that were elected

---

[1] "The men of North Carolina were the first in America to declare their independence of Great Britain, and the most resolute in defending it."—Johnson's *Traditions of the Revolution*, 551.

"It will forever redound to the honour of North Carolina that it was among her people that the bold idea of Independence was first conceived and proclaimed to the world; and this early manifestation of patriotic enthusiasm never knew diminution."—Garden's *Anecdotes of the Revolution*, 2d Series, III, 7, 9.

[2] "Within a few weeks after Moore's Creek, nearly 9,000 citizens of the Colony organized in behalf of the common cause of Colonial independence. It is worthy of note that North Carolina ever after was conspicuously faithful to her obligations."—Carrington's *Battles of the Revolution*, 174.

"The patriots derived an immense advantage from the victory at Moore's Creek. The North Carolinians learned to know their own strength. They had combated with success the Regulators and the Scotch, who had appeared to them at first so formidable; and in the space of ten days they had assembled 10,000 men full of courage and resolution."—Botta's *Hist. of the War of Independence*, I, 324.

to the Continental Congress. Her troops were the first from the South to join Washington at Cambridge, and, her own borders being free from invasion, she fought for the defence of every sister Province from Massachussetts to Georgia.[1] In Baltimore were fitted out the first cruisers, which were the pioneers of the American navy.[2] The first suggestion of Washington as commander-in-chief came from Thomas Johnson, afterwards Governor of republican Maryland; "without whom," said John Adams, "there would have been no revolution," and whose political sagacity was such, that the Maryland Convention withdrew his appointment as General, that the country might not lose the benefit of his wisdom in the council-chamber. Limited as was her population, Maryland furnished more than 20,000 men to the revolutionary army, and her quota was generally fuller than that of the other Provinces. Probably none of them contributed so liberally both in men and in supplies.

Everywhere, throughout the war, are found the brave soldiers of these two States; there are few

---

[1] "From 1776, before Boston, and through the entire war, the States of Maryland and Delaware were represented on nearly every battle-field. Although their troops were few in numbers, they were distinguished for valour."—Carrington's *Battles*, 491.

[2] "Joshua Barney, of Maryland, was the first of the naval officers of our country who engaged in the service,—he was the last to quit it."—Garden's *Anecdotes*, 2d Series, III, 94.

battle-fields, from the Hudson river to the Savannah, which were not watered with the best blood of Maryland and North Carolina; and when the latter Province was threatened with subjugation by Lord Cornwallis, it was the Maryland Line that came to her rescue, and formed under Greene the heart of that army which was to strike a fatal blow at British supremacy in America.

But has history done full justice to these men? With few exceptions, most certainly not. They might proudly say: "we make history and others write it;" but the practical result is that many a Carolina child knows all about Bunker Hill and very little of Moore's Creek; many a Maryland boy will recount the incidents of the "Boston Tea-party," while mainly ignorant of the burning of the Peggy Stewart. When Johnson published his life of Gen. Greene seventy years ago, when therefore many of the actors in the revolutionary drama were still on the stage, he said:—"There is a clannish spirit in the States of the Union which will ever dispose the writers they produce, to blazon with peculiar zeal the virtues and talents of the eminent men of their respective States. And it will probably happen, that in future times the States that have produced the ablest writers will enjoy the reputation of having produced the ablest statesmen, generals and orators."[1] Words truly prophetic, and it is pre-eminently the duty of the men of our generation to right these historic wrongs.

The spirit of resistance to tyranny and to unjust legislation was early rife in the Colony of the Calverts, and in October 1774 the brig Peggy Stewart with her cargo of tea was burned at Annapolis, in open day, by men who boldly assumed the responsibility of their act. During the following winter active preparations were made for the inevitable conflict, and when the news of Lexington came, Smallwood was put in command of a battalion of seven companies at Baltimore, while two companies of riflemen from Western Maryland were hurried forward to take part in the siege of Boston.

The little Province was contributing prodigally to the cause, and of her best. "We are sending all that can be armed and equipped;" reported the Maryland Council of Safety on August 16th, "and the people of New York, for whom we have great affection, can have no more than our all."[2] The recruits were young enthusiasts, who represented the first families of the State. "The city-bred Marylander was distinguished by the most fashionably cut coat, the most macaroni cocked hat, and hottest blood in the Union; if there was any exception, it was to be found among the children of

[1] Johnson's *Life of Gen. Greene*, II, 181.
[2] Force's *American Archives*, 5th Series, I, 975.

the sun of a still more Southern location."[1] In July 1776, Smallwood's Macaronis, in their brilliant uniform of buff and scarlet, joined Washington's army at New York, and at the battle of Long Island, on August 27th, the men of the Maryland Line for a while held at bay the entire British left wing, covering the American retreat with a loss of nearly half their own number, and beginning thus splendidly that career, which was to close five years later, in the gallant bayonet charge at Eutaw Springs.

What a task was imposed upon these young, untried soldiers! Five times did these brave boys, but 400 in number, charge a brigade of British infantry; for hours had they to meet the "push of the bayonet,"—that dread even of the hardiest veterans.—unsustained too by the stimulus of possible victory; for all that could be hoped for was to protect the retreat and save the American army from annihilation. Our troops had been forced to yield at every point, and " none remained in the field but Stirling with the regiment of Maryland and that of Delaware. For nearly four hours they stood in their ranks with colours flying; when Stirling, perceiving the main body of the British army rapidly coming behind him, gave the word to retreat. They withdrew in perfect order. The only avenue of escape was by wading

---

[1] Graydon's Memoirs, 180.

through Gowanus creek; and this passage was almost cut off by troops under Cornwallis. Stirling must hold Cornwallis in check, or his whole party is lost: he ordered the Delaware regiment and one-half of that of Maryland to make the best of their way across the marsh and creek, while he confronted the advancing British with only five companies of Marylanders. The young soldiers flew at the enemy with unparalleled bravery, in view of all the American generals and troops within the lines, who alternately praised and pitied them. Washington wrung his hands, as he exclaimed: 'My God! what brave men must I this day lose!' When forced to give way, they rallied and renewed the onset. In this manner ten minutes were gained, so that the Delawares with their prisoners, and half the Maryland regiment passed the creek. The devoted men who had saved them were beaten back by masses of troops, and cut to pieces or taken; only nine succeeded in escaping."[1]

Throughout the campaign of '76 the Marylanders sustained the brilliant reputation won at Long Island, and Adjutant-General Reed declared that "the gallantry of the Southern men has inspired the whole army."[2] At 'Harlem Heights they carried the British intrenchments at the

---

[1] Bancroft's *U. S.*, V, 32.   [2] Reed's *Life of Reed*, I, 221.

point of the bayonet: at White Plains they resisted an overwhelming force with the loss of a hundred men: in the retreat across New Jersey they were prominent in every action: so that in the four months between the battles of Long Island and Princeton the old Maryland Line was almost annihilated.

In the summer of 1777 the soldiers of the North Carolina Line joined the army of Washington. They arrived laurel-crowned, for the defeat of Lord Dunmore at Norfolk[1] in December 1775, and for the part which they had borne in the brilliant defence of Charleston in June 1776, against the combined fleet and army of Admiral Sir Peter Parker and Sir Henry Clinton. This Southern campaign was so successful[2] that for nearly three years the Carolinas were free from the presence of the enemy; and had it failed, it is difficult to see how the other Colonies could have brought the Revolution to a triumphant conclusion. General Charles Lee, chief in command at Charleston, re-

---

[1] The Virginia Convention at Williamsburg, on Dec. 22, 1775, resolved, "That the thanks of this Convention are justly due to the brave officers, gentlemen volunteers, and soldiers of North Carolina, as well as to our brethren of that Province in general, for their prompt and generous aid in defence of our common rights against the enemies of America."—North Carolina *Colonial Records*, Vol. X, p. xi.

[2] The obstinate resistance of the Virginians, and the disasters of the partisans of England in North Carolina, precluded all hope of success in these two provinces."—Botta, I, 334.

ported of his troops that "their conduct is such as
does them the highest honour: no man ever did, and
it is impossible ever can, behave better. The South
and North Carolinians that we have here are admirable soldiers. I know not which corps I have
the greatest reason to be pleased with, Muhlenberg's
Virginians or the North Carolina troops; they are
both equally alert, zealous and spirited."[1] On their
march northward through Virginia, the victors were
greeted with enthusiasm; for fame had gone before
them of their gallantry, which had helped to baffle
an attack that was as bravely and skilfully conducted as any in the annals of naval warfare.

Arrived at Washington's entrenched camp at
Middlebrook in June, the North Carolina brigade
was placed under command of Stirling, and on
Sept. 11th took part with his division in the battle
of the Brandywine. The American forces in this
campaign were but 8,000, while the enemy mus-
tered 30,000.[2] On October 4th, at Germantown,—
a field on which all the thirteen Colonies were represented,—the Maryland brigade, and the North
Carolinians under Nash,—who fell at the head of
his troops,[3]—fought side by side, constituting the

[1] Moultrie's *Memoirs of the Revolution*, I, 170. *The Lee Papers*, N. Y. Hist. Soc., II, 93, 102.

[2] Stedman's *Hist. of Amer. War*, I, 284.

[3] "One of the most lamented losses at Germantown was that of General Nash, of North Carolina."—Botta, II, 47.

right wing of the army immediately under the eye of Washington, of which he reported to Congress that "both officers and men behaved with a degree of gallantry that did them the highest credit."[1] Brandywine and Germantown are the first battles in which the troops of the two States are brought into helpful contact, and here begins that honourable rivalry for distinction which was to last throughout the war. At Monmouth, Camden, King's Mountain, Cowpens, Guilford, Hobkirk's Hill, Eutaw Springs,—it is on the Marylanders, or the North Carolinians, or upon both, that falls the chief brunt of the battle; and it is upon the conduct of the men of these two Colonies, upon their steady valour or liability to panic, that turns the issue of victory or defeat.

At Germantown Maryland's favorite hero, John Eager Howard, first found an opportunity for the display of his great soldierly qualities. He had served as Captain in the regiment of Col. Carvil Hall; had joined the Continental army in time to take part in the battle of White Plains; and was promoted Major in one of the seven Continental regiments. In the absence of the Colonel and Lieut.-Colonel he was in command of his regiment at Germantown, where he displayed alike great skill and courage. Garden, one of Lee's legionaries, who served with Howard in the South,

---

[1] Sparks's *Washington*, V, 80.

ascribes to him "every requisite for the perfection of the military character,—patience, judgment, intrepidity, decision:" and after the campaign in the Carolinas Gen. Greene said, "He is as good an officer as the world affords, and deserves a statue of gold no less than the Roman and Grecian heroes."[1]

A fortnight after Germantown, the surrender of Burgoyne brought about an exchange of prisoners, and this released for active service another great Maryland soldier, Otho Holland Williams. He had served at the siege of Boston in 1775, as Lieutenant and Captain in the first company of Marylanders that was sent to Massachusetts. When the Maryland and Virginia riflemen were formed into a regiment in 1776, he was promoted Major, modestly declining the appointment of Colonel of the Frederick County battalion, as diffident of his ability to discharge the duties of so high a rank. He was taken prisoner at the surrender of Fort Washington, where the Marylanders sustained a long and bloody conflict with a body of Hessians more than ten times their number. The harsh and unworthy treatment which Williams received at the hands of the British, during his fifteen months of captivity, permanently impaired his health, but fortunately did not deprive his country of his invaluable ser-

[1] Garden's *Anecdotes*, 60 and 61.

vices; and with his advancement to the Coloneley of the 6th regiment of the Maryland Line begins that brilliant career which has shed so much lustre on his native State.

In the campaign of the following year, 1778, the Maryland and North Carolina troops were conspicuous; and at Monmouth, on June 28th, the North Carolinians stationed on the left wing saved it from being outflanked by Lord Cornwallis, while at a critical moment of the battle, the safety of the army, as at Long Island, depended upon the steadiness and courage of the Maryland Line. Gen. Charles Lee, who commanded the advance corps, failed to carry out Washington's order to attack the British on the march, and retreated; on which account he was afterwards court-martialed for disobedience of orders and misbehaviour before the enemy. This strange misconduct endangered the whole army, and in the emergency Washington turned to Colonels Stewart and Ramsay of the Maryland Line to hold the British army in check until he could rally his own. "We will check them" was Ramsay's proud reply, and Stewart being wounded early in the action, the command of the Marylanders devolved upon him. He fought every inch of ground with desperate obstinacy, and for some minutes held back the whole British Line; until left almost without troops, and dangerously wounded in a hand-to-hand encounter with several dragoons, he was taken prisoner. The point was gained ; the enemy's advance was checked, and Gen. Clinton paid a fitting tribute to Ramsay's heroism by promptly releasing him on parole.

No important battle signalized the campaign of 1779; but it was marked by one very gallant enterprise, the capture of Stony Point on the Hudson,[1] in which the troops both of Maryland and North Carolina bore a most honourable part. Gen. Lee wrote to Wayne:—" Your assault on Stony Point is not only the most brilliant throughout the whole course of the war on either side, but one of the most brilliant I am acquainted with in history."[2] The British occupation of this post threatened West Point, and Washington formed a plan for its capture, the execution of which he intrusted to Gen. Wayne, who, on the evening of July 15th, secretly drew near the fort with a small body of the choicest troops of the army. The Marylanders under him were commanded by Major Stewart, and the battalion of North Carolinians by Major Murfree.

The position was considered impregnable, as it is a bold bluff accessible only by a narrow causeway,

---

[1] " It was an enterprise of difficulty and danger; and Gen. Wayne, who commanded it, deserved great praise for his gallantry and good conduct, as did the troops which he commanded for their bravery."—Stedman's *Hist. of the American War*, II, 145.

[2] *Lee Papers*, III, 357.

which is overflowed at high water. Strong breastworks crowned the hill, which was encircled by a double row of abatis; while the garrison consisted of six hundred veterans well supplied with artillery. At midnight Wayne moved silently upon the fort; Major Stewart leading a corps of 100 volunteers with unloaded muskets on the left, and Lieut.-Col. Fleury a similar column on the right. Murfree's men in the centre advanced by the road up the slope directly in front of the works, keeping up an incessant fire to distract the attention of the garrison from the other storming parties; or, as Wayne expressed it, "to *amuse* the enemy in front,"—an amusement, however, which would draw upon them the concentrated fire of the fort. In front of the American line were two small bodies of twenty picked men, called the forlorn hope. led by Lieutenants Gibbons and Knox. Armed with axes, their task was to remove the abatis and other obstructions for the assaulting party. The danger attending this duty is shown by the fact that seventeen of Gibbons's little company of twenty. and more than half of Knox's, were killed or wounded; yet both officers and men were so emulous of the honour of serving in the forlorn hope, that the choice of them had to be decided by lot.

The Americans were very near the works before their approach was discovered. "Come on, ye damned rebels; come on!" shouted the enemy;

to which some of our men replied, "Don't be in such a hurry, my lads; we will be with you presently." They were met by a terrific fire of grape and musketry, but they dashed on without hesitation, and in a few minutes the right and left columns entered the fort almost at the same time, and met in the centre. Major Murfree conducted admirably his part of the attack, and his two companies were the only troops that fired a gun. Lieut. Col. Fleury was the first to spring upon the ramparts, and seizing the colours of the post he shouted the watchword "The fort's our own." At the same moment, Stewart with the left column entered from the opposite side, and Murfree's detachment as bravely seized other portions of the works.[1]

The garrison surrendered at once, begging for quarter, which was magnanimously granted; not a blow was struck after resistance ceased.[2] "The fort and garrison are ours." was Wayne's laconic despatch to Washington, dated July 16th, 2 A. M. "Our officers and men behaved like men determined to be free;" and in his later reports and

[1] Washington said, "The assault of Stony Point does much honour to the troops employed in it, as no men could behave better. Every officer and man of the corps deserves great credit."—Ford's *Writings of Washington*, VII, 499, and VIII, 1.

[2] "The conduct of the Americans was highly meritorious, for they would have been fully justified in putting the garrison to the sword."—Stedman, II, 145.

letters he pays a fitting tribute to the heroism and good conduct of Murfree, Stewart, and the other leaders of his various detachments. Among the younger officers too were many conspicuous examples of personal gallantry. Lieutenant Knox was the first to follow Fleury into the enemy's works; Lieutenant Gibbons was breveted Captain for his heroism; and Lieutenant Daves of the 2nd North Carolina, who had won promotion by his conduct at Germantown, was desperately wounded while bravely leading one of the storming parties of volunteers.

The news of the capture of the fort was received with the greatest enthusiasm throughout the country. Stony Point was the first strongly entrenched post which our troops ventured to attack; and the brilliant success came to inspire hope at a moment when disaster was threatening the cause of independence.

II.

In the early years of the Revolution the struggle was chiefly confined to the Northern Provinces; but Monmouth is the last battle of note fought on Northern soil. The tide of war then turned southward: the Southern Colonies became the scene of decisive contest, and within their borders was definitely settled the question of British supremacy or American independence. The plan of the enemy was to subdue Georgia, and then, extending their conquest northward, to form a junction in Virginia or Maryland with Sir Henry Clinton's forces from New York, and thus bring the whole Atlantic seaboard under the dominion of the King. Lord George Germain, Secretary of State for the Colonies, wrote to Lord Cornwallis:—"It is the King's firm purpose to recover the Southern Provinces in preference to all others, and to push the war from South to North, securing what is conquered as we go on."[1]

On December 29th, 1778, Savannah was captured, and in the course of the following year the British completed the subjugation of Georgia, and entered upon the conquest of South Carolina. To Gen. Lincoln was assigned the defence of Charleston, the most important city in the South, and in November 1779, the North Carolina Continentals under Gen. Hogun were ordered to reinforce him. This gallant brigade, reduced by the arduous campaigns under Washington from 5000 to 700 men, set out for the long march from their cantonments on the Hudson. It was a terrible winter journey in the then condition of things:[2] the troops suf-

[1] Clinton-Cornwallis Controversy, II, 11.

[2] Washington wrote Lafayette:—"The extreme cold, the deep snows, and other impediments, retarded the march of the North Carolina Brigade. The oldest people now living do not remember so hard a winter. The severity of the frost exceeded anything of the kind that had ever been experienced in this climate before."—Ford's *Writings of Washington*, VIII, 220.

fered greatly, and did not reach their destination till March 13th, 1780.

After the failure of "The Grand Model," Locke and Shaftesbury's philosophic Constitution for Carolina, the Province was divided; and two generations of independent existence had already stamped upon the old North State the permanent characteristics, which distinguish her from her Virginia neighbours on the North and the Huguenot settlers on the South. On previous occasions in the war she had come to the rescue of her sister Province, and on February 24th, 1779, Charles Pinckney wrote: "We have upwards of 3000 North Carolina troops with us, and I esteem this as the most convincing proof of their zeal for the glorious cause. They have been so willing and ready on all occasions to afford us all the assistance in their power, that I shall ever love a North Carolinian, and join with Gen. Moultrie in confessing that they have been the salvation of this country."[1]

To save Charleston was of supreme importance,[2] and in the Spring of 1780 Washington determined

[1] *N. C. Univ. Magazine*, April, 1878. Schenck's *North Carolina* in 1780-1781, p. 35.

See also Johnson's *Traditions of the Revolution*, 308:—"North Carolina generously sent her troops whenever called for, to join in our battles, and aid in our defence."

[2] Washington wrote Lincoln:—"If the British succeed against Charleston, there is much reason to believe that the Southern States will become the principal theatre of the war."—Ford's *Washington*, VIII, 248.

to send to Lincoln his favorite troops, the soldiers of the Maryland Line, then about 2000 in number, or nearly one-fifth of his little army. Baron de Kalb was placed in command, and on April 16th they set out from the camp at Morristown; but before they crossed the Virginia line Charleston had fallen. Lincoln made the fatal mistake of allowing himself to be shut up in the city; so that when he was forced to surrender, on May 12th, the loss to the American cause was not merely the Southern Capital, but many of the best soldiers of the Continental army. North Carolina lost 59 Line officers, nearly all of her regulars, and a thousand of her disciplined militia. At a moment when the country could ill spare one of her defenders, the veteran soldiers of the Carolinas, penned in British prison ships, were perishing miserably of disease and despair.

With the fall of Charleston all organized resistance ceased in South Carolina; the strongholds of Camden, Beaufort and Ninety-Six surrendered, and some men of mark counselled submission. Sir Henry Clinton considered the Province as so completely subdued, that he issued a proclamation requiring all men within his lines to take up arms for the king; an unwise act which drove all would-be neutrals into the rebel ranks. "If we must fight," said they, "let it be on the side of America, our friends and countrymen."[1] Before setting out for New York, he wrote, on June 4th, to Lord Germain, "There are few men in South Carolina who are not either our prisoners or in the army with us; and I dare entertain hopes that Earl Cornwallis's presence on the frontier of North Carolina, will call back the inhabitants of that Province from their state of error and disobedience."[2]

He left Cornwallis in command, and at the end of June the latter reported that all resistance was at an end in Georgia and South Carolina, and that he would proceed to subdue North Carolina as soon as the harvest was gathered.

The disaster seemed indeed a fatal one. "We look on America as at our feet," was the exultant exclamation of Horace Walpole, when the news of Lincoln's surrender reached London. But the veterans of the Maryland Line were already on the march to replace those that had been lost at Charleston, and to rescue the Southern Provinces from the enemy. They reached Hillsborough on June 22nd, to find North Carolina not only stripped of her veteran troops, but without the means to fitly arm the men that she was able to bring into the field. "The North Carolinians were always active and ready to defend their country, but they were badly provided with arms;

---

[1] Moultrie's *Memoirs*, II, 210.
[2] Tarleton's *Campaigns of 1780 and 1781*, pp. 82, 83.

they were obliged to form their scythes and sickles into swords and spears. Yet the North Carolina militia were a very great check to the British, and stopped their rapid progress over North and South Carolina."[1] More volunteers offered their services than could be equipped. The Tories too were organizing, and measures had to be taken to meet an enemy within as well as without the borders of the State.

The name Tory still lingers as a term of opprobrium; but has not the time come to do justice to the Loyalists of our Revolution? Our enthusiastic admiration for the patriots, whose courage and endurance achieved our independence, has hitherto blinded us to the virtues of their opponents. But more than a century has passed since those days of bitter strife, and we of this generation should be able to judge impartially the men who believed it their duty to uphold the royal authority. Generous loyalty to a sovereign is as lofty a sentiment as love of liberty, and prompts to as noble deeds of devotion and self-sacrifice.

In the forum of public opinion nothing justifies a man in taking service under a foreign enemy against his own country, and even so illustrious an example as that of Moreau forms no exception; his memory is not held in honour, and an atmosphere

[1] Moultrie's *Memoirs*, II, 213.

of pathetic sadness hovers over his lonely grave among the Saxon hills. But in a civil war the question is very different, as was well illustrated in our recent struggle. There are probably men within the sound of my voice who fought on different sides in that contest, and whose conscientiousness and patriotism no one can impugn. They are praiseworthy or blameworthy, not for the choice of the flag under which they marched, but for the motives which prompted that choice, and the deeds that justified it. Many a Tory in our Revolution lived a life of heroic sacrifice, and died a martyr to the cause which claimed his loyal devotion.

The men of Maryland entered upon their great task in the South with resolution, though it must have appeared almost impossible of accomplishment. Col. Howard afterwards said of the campaign: " our march to the southward seemed to be a forlorn hope." Another happy illustration of the truth uttered by our great poet that

"Things out of hope are compassed oft with venturing."[1]

De Kalb's first impressions of the old North State are ludicrously unpleasant. In a letter to his wife of June 21st, just after he had crossed the frontier, he says : " I am suffering from intolerable heat, and the most voracious of insects of every hue

[1] *Venus and Adonis*, 567.

and form. Of the violence of thunder storms in this part of the world Europeans cannot form any idea."[1]

Though without proper food, clothing, or arms for her troops, North Carolina was making strenuous efforts to repel the British invasion, and just at the time when the Marylanders entered her borders, the victory of June 20th over the Tories at Ramsour's Mill, the successes of Major Davie near Hanging Rock, and the exploits of the mountaineers under Shelby and McDowell, had inspired the patriots with fresh hope and courage.

With a leader like De Kalb, the Maryland veterans and North Carolina recruits might have marched to assured victory; but he was unfortunately superseded by Gen. Gates, to whom the surrender of Burgoyne had given a factitious reputation. Gates took command at Buffalo Ford on Deep River, July 25th, and at once showed his lack of wise judgment by declining to provide a sufficient force of cavalry, and resolving to march by the direct route to Camden; though this led through a district where the Tories were active, and which was too barren and uncultivated to furnish food for the army; while the more circuitous road lay through the fertile counties of Rowan and Mecklenburg, whose people were zealous in the cause.

The sufferings of the troops on this march were great, and Col. Otho Williams said of his stout-

[1] Kapp's *Life of De Kalb*, 200.

hearted Marylanders that "they gave early proofs of that patient submission, inflexible fortitude, and undeviating integrity, which they afterwards more eminently displayed."[1] In the scarcity of food the men lived chiefly on unripe fruit, which produced much sickness, and the officers resorted to the expedient of using their hair-powder to thicken the meagre soup.

Gates approached Camden without obtaining any definite information about the enemy, who however were well apprized of all his movements. Cornwallis had arrived with reinforcements from Charleston without Gates's knowledge, and while the Americans were on a night march with the purpose of surprising and overwhelming Lord Rawdon's command, they unexpectedly met the united forces of the enemy advancing to attack them. After a brief skirmish the two armies drew apart to await the dawn.

It was August 16th, the day of Camden, the most disastrous in the annals of the Revolution: a day of undying glory for Maryland, on account of the admirable conduct of her troops, but one that then seemed fatal to the independence of the Southern Provinces. Cornwallis believed that this brilliant success removed the last obstacle from his path of victory across North Carolina.

[1] Johnson's *Greene*, I, 488.

The disposition of his troops on the field was admirable: the left wing was commanded by Lord Rawdon; the right by Col. Webster, with Tarleton's cavalry in the rear; while both flanks were protected by swamps. De Kalb's division, consisting of the second Maryland brigade under Gen. Gist, and the Delaware regiment, faced Rawdon; the North Carolinians under Caswell formed the centre of the line, and the left wing was composed of the newly enrolled Virginia militia under Stevens; the Americans thus having "their best troops on the side strongest by nature, the worst on the weakest."[1] Two hundred yards in the rear was stationed the first Maryland brigade under Smallwood as a reserve corps.

At the opening of the engagement Col. Otho Williams, with a small body of volunteers, advanced in front of the American line, to draw the enemy's fire and to encourage the militia; but before Webster's impetuous charge, supported by cavalry, the raw recruits broke and fled in hopeless confusion. Dixon's regiment of North Carolinians alone held its ground, and upon them and Gist's Marylanders fell the weight of the whole British line. Never did men behave more gallantly; nowhere can be found more brilliant instances of personal courage, or examples of more perfect discipline; but the British fought with equal

[1] Bancroft, V, 387.

bravery, and the odds were overwhelmingly in their favour.

De Kalb, who exposed himself recklessly, and led a successful charge upon Rawdon's division, fell into the enemy's hands mortally wounded. His dying words were a tribute to the exemplary conduct of his soldiers, which "gave him an endearing sense of the merits of the troops which he had the honour to command."[1] Nearly half of his men were killed or captured, the remainder escaping to the friendly shelter of the swamps. Major Anderson kept together a small body of the Second Maryland regiment, and Col. Howard gathered some stragglers in the woods.[2] In three days they, together with Smallwood, Gist. Hall and Gunby, succeeded in reaching Charlotte, 60 miles distant, and when Howard was asked what subsistence they had found, he replied simply "some peaches." Gen. Gates had arrived at Charlotte on the night after the battle, and passing on to Hillsborough he gave orders for the scattered remnant of the troops to rendezvous there.

From the camp in New Jersey, on October 13th, Gen. Knox wrote to Gen. Smallwood to inquire how he sustained the "fatigues and hardships of

---

[1] Kapp's *Life of De Kalb*, 237.

[2] "Complete as was the dispersion of our army at Camden, the Maryland and Delaware troops gained imperishable laurels for their conduct. Nor is it possible to withhold from Col. Dixon, of North Carolina, the most unqualified applause."—Paul Allen's *Amer. Rev.*, II, 323.

war in a Southern climate. I suppose you must find it agreeable in some degree, as it has produced you such a harvest of glory. The affair at Camden will not be more remarkable for its adverse circumstances than for the firm gallantry of the Maryland troops. The veterans of the army here admire their conduct, and ardently wish to have been in such numbers, side by side with their old companions, as to have enabled them to gain a victory which their bravery so richly merited."[1]

Lee pays a flattering tribute to the valour and steadiness of the troops:—

"The Marylanders, with Dixon's North Carolina regiment, although greatly outnumbered, firmly maintained the desperate conflict. The brigade, borne down by superior numbers, rallied again and again; but finally the intrepid Marylanders were compelled to give up the unequal contest. More than a third of the Continental troops were killed or wounded. The North Carolina militia also suffered greatly; more than 300 of them were taken and 100 were killed and wounded. None can withhold applause from Col. Dixon and his North Carolina regiment of militia. Having their flank exposed by the flight of the other militia, they turned with disdain from the ignoble example; and fixing their eyes on the Marylanders, whose left flank they became, determined to vie in

[1] Balch's *Maryland Papers*, 116.

deeds of courage with their veteran comrades. In
every vicissitude of the battle this regiment maintained
its ground, and when the reserve under
Smallwood relieved its naked flank, forced the
enemy to fall back."[1]

No battle of the war put to a severer test the
mettle of our men, and the disorderly retreat was
marked by every incident of picturesque and
pathetic distress. Col. Otho Williams said that
"a just representation of it would exhibit an image
of compound wretchedness: care, anxiety, pain,
poverty, hurry, confusion, humiliation and dejection
would be characteristic traits in the mortifying
picture."[2]

The defeat at Camden indeed marks the darkest
hour of the Revolution; but it proved to be that
darkness which heralds the coming dawn, and for
the happy change in our country's fortune we
owe much to the soldiers of Maryland. For many
months disaster had followed disaster in the South,
and in the North there had been no compensating
victory. The hearts of the patriots were heavy
with anxiety, and the enemy was exultant in the
confidence of success. Lord Germain wrote to Sir
Henry Clinton:—"So very contemptible is the
rebel force in all its parts, and so vast is our superiority
everywhere, that no resistance on their part

[1] Lee's *Memoirs of the War in the Southern Department*, 184-187.
[2] Johnson's *Greene*, I, 501.

is to be apprehended that can materially obstruct the progress of the King's army in the speedy suppression of the rebellion."[1]

Throughout the Colonies there was every reason for great discouragement. The government paper money had so depreciated in value that the people were almost without a circulating medium. As the area of the conflict extended more and more widely, the difficulty of communication became embarrassing in the extreme. The supply, not only of arms, but of food and clothing for the troops, had become in some cases a problem impossible of solution. North Carolina, to whose territory the struggle was about to be transferred, besides the loss at Charleston of her regulars and many of her militia, was bereft at Camden of some of her most valuable officers.

In this disheartening condition of public affairs came the startling tidings of Arnold's treason, which seemed to fill to the brim the cup of national calamity. No wonder that Otho Williams should write to Col. Morgan in vigorous alliterative phrase: "What do you think of the damnable doings of that diabolical dog Arnold?"[2]

It was plain that some prompt and decisive step must be taken, or the cause was lost. The emergency demanded a leader of different calibre from

[1] Clinton-Cornwallis Controversy, I, 335.
[2] Graham's *Life of Morgan*, 244.

that of Gates or Lincoln, and Washington found
him in his trusty Lieutenant, Nathanael Greene.
Second in military capacity only to his great chief-
tain, Greene is alike conspicuous for his merit and
his modesty. When informed of his appointment
to the supreme command in the South, he wrote to
Washington: "I lament that my abilities are not
more competent to the duties that will be required
of me. But as far as zeal and attention can supply
the defect, I flatter myself my country will have
little cause to complain."[1] His grateful country
has ever acknowledged that, so far from giving
cause for complaint, his masterly conduct of the
brilliant campaign in the Carolinas has filled her
heart with pride and thankfulness.

What was thought of him by his contemporaries
is seen in the encomium of the Chevalier de la
Luzerne, French ambassador at that time to the
United Colonies: "Other Generals subdue their
enemy by the means with which their country or
sovereign furnishes them; but Greene appears to
subdue his enemy by his own means. He conquers
by magic. History furnishes no parallel to this."[2]
He was in the prime of his powers when he
assumed command at Charlotte, on December 4th,
1780; thirty-eight years of age, and in the full
vigour of ripe manhood. All his faculties had
been trained by four years of arduous experience,

[1] Greene's *Life of Gen. Greene*, II, 374.   [2] Garden's *Anecdotes*, 77.

and his temper admirably combined the prudence of age with the hopeful enthusiasm of youth.

III.

After the rout at Camden the scattered troops were gathered at Salisbury, and then marched to Hillsborough, where the army was reorganized. Here Gates received reinforcements of the Virginia Line, and with them came Col. Daniel Morgan, "who never gave other than the wisest counsels, and stood first for conduct, effective leadership, and unsurpassable courage on the field of battle. He was at that time the ablest commander of light troops in the world, for in no European army of that day were there troops like those which he trained."[1] Gates assigned to him a special light corps of infantry, and the cavalry troop of Col. Wm. Washington; North Carolina furnishing the command with clothing. The Marylanders being now reduced in numbers to less than 800, the several regiments of the old Line were amalgamated into one, under Williams and Howard as Colonel and Lieut.-Colonel, and called the First Maryland. Col. Williams pays a high tribute to the fidelity and discipline of these troops in the camp at Hillsborough. All despondency disappeared, and the men grew eager again to face the

[1] Bancroft, V, 191, 480.

enemy; even the invalids refusing to be left behind, when, after two months of recuperation, the army set out on November 2nd for Charlotte.

North Carolina was meanwhile labouring earnestly to repair her great losses, responding nobly to every demand on her for men and supplies. Her gratitude for help given by Maryland was shown by creating Smallwood Major-General, and placing him in supreme command of her militia. The latter were already assembling under Generals Sumner and Davidson, full of hope and spirit. Within a fortnight after Camden, Major Davie declared that the militia, if aided by " a small body of regulars, would still keep the enemy at bay;"[1] and Otho Williams said that the conduct at this crisis of " the patriots of Mecklenburg and Waxhaws entitles them to a whole page of eulogium in the best history that shall record the circumstances of the Revolution."[2]

In September Lord Cornwallis entered North Carolina, expecting a welcome from numerous Loyalists, who would strew with flowers his path of conquest. But the defence of Charlotte by the young heroes, Davie and Graham, who with a mere handful of men checked for a while the advance of the whole British army, showed him, to use his own expressive phrase, that he had run into " a Hornet's nest;" and his foraging officers reported

[1] *N. C. Univ. Mag.*, V, 184.   [2] Johnson's *Greene*, I, 502.

that they found "a rebel in every bush outside of the lines of the encampment."[1]

Keen must have been his disappointment in finding this temper of the people, for he afterwards wrote to Lord Germain: "The great object of our arduous campaign is the calling forth the numerous Loyalists of North Carolina; but the numbers of our friends in the Province are not so great as had been represented, and their friendship is only passive; not over two hundred have been prevailed upon to follow us." and the march to the Yadkin was through "one of the most rebellious tracts in America."[2]

Tarleton's words are an equally emphatic tribute to the persistent patriotism of the North Carolinians:—"The counties of Mecklenburg and Rowan were more hostile to England than any others in America. No British commander could obtain any information which would facilitate his designs or guide his future conduct. Notwithstanding the different checks and losses sustained by the militia of the district, they continued their hostilities with unwearied perseverance."[3] All classes shared the patriotic enthusiasm, and the

[1] Cooke's *Rev. Hist. of N. C.*, 168.
An intercepted letter of Cornwallis's aid-de-camp describes Charlotte at this time as "an agreeable village, but in a damned rebellious country."— Moore's *Diary of the Rev.*, II, 352.
[2] Clinton-Cornwallis Controversy, I, 358, 362, 417.
[3] Tarleton's *Campaigns*, 163, 164.

young ladies of Mecklenburg and Rowan entered into a pledge not to receive the attentions of young men who would not volunteer in defence of their country.[1]

But it was not merely a hostile spirit that the people showed; a decisive battle was to mark the turn in the tide of misfortune, and be the harbinger of future victories. When Cornwallis entered North Carolina, he detached on special service his brilliant partisan leader, Col. Ferguson. He was to bring into subjection to British rule the bold pioneers beyond the Alleghanies, the "overmountain men," as they were called. A messenger was despatched to them demanding submission, and threatening them and their homes with fire and sword. The sturdy frontiers-men promptly accepted the challenge, and under the leadership of Shelby, Sevier, McDowell and others, determined to cross the mountains and meet Ferguson on his own ground. To the 700 North Carolinians were added 400 South Carolinians and Virginians; Col. Campbell was put in command by vote of his fellow officers, and they came up with the enemy on October 7th. Ferguson had pitched his camp on King's Mountain, whence he said "all the rebels out of hell could not drive him." The opposing forces were about equal in number, and both were without cavalry or artillery. The enemy had the

[1] Lossing's *Field Book of the Revolution*, II, 420.

advantage of the bayonet; the mountain-men had their trusty rifles, a more dangerous weapon from the nature of the ground. It was a contest of Whig and Tory, not of American and British. The Whigs surrounded the mountain, and drew gradually near their prey from all quarters. The enemy fought with desperate courage; but they fell by scores before the deadly rifle of the mountaineers,[1] and when Ferguson was struck down, the little remnant of his men, surrounded and overwhelmed, surrendered. None escaped: the battle had lasted only an hour, but the fight was fierce from the outset, and little quarter was given. The king's army of a thousand men was annihilated, with a loss to the Whigs of less than one hundred.

The effect of this brilliant success was far-reaching; victory had again perched upon the banners of the patriots, and hope and confidence cheered their hearts.[2] Again had the valour of the sons of North Carolina turned the tide of invasion from her border; they had checked the advance of Cornwallis, just as in '76, at Moore's Creek, they had

[1] "King's Mountain, as well as many other battles, proves that the militia are brave men, and will fight if you let them come to action in their own way. The charge of the bayonet it can never be expected that undisciplined troops could stand."—Moultrie's *Memoirs*, II, 245.

[2] Washington wrote to Gov. Nash :—"The success of the militia against Col. Ferguson will awaken more extensively that spirit of bravery and enterprise, which displayed itself so conspicuously on the occasion."—Ford's *Writings of Washington*, IX, 18.

baffled Sir Henry Clinton's plans of invasion. Congress expressed a high appreciation of the good conduct of the troops, and Gen. Gates declared that their "glorious behaviour in the action will transmit their names to posterity with the highest honours and applause."[1] The victory at King's Mountain, which, "in the spirit of the American soldiers, was like the rising at Concord, in its effect like the success at Bennington, changed the aspects of the war. It quickened the Legislature of North Carolina to earnest efforts. It encouraged Virginia to devote her resources to the country south of her border. Cornwallis had hoped to step with ease from one Carolina to the other, and from those to the conquest of Virginia, and he had now no other choice but to retreat."[2]

He immediately broke up camp at Charlotte, and retired to Winnsboro, seventy miles southward, to await reinforcements; abandoning his plan of a winter campaign in North Carolina. Morgan's corps appeared soon after in the neighbourhood of Camden; but Gates recalled him to Charlotte, where he had established his headquarters.

It was at this juncture that Gen. Greene arrived on December 2d, and took command of the army, consisting then of about a thousand Continentals and as many militia. Most of the regulars were

[1] Draper's *King's Mountain*, 374.   [2] Bancroft, V, 400.

the Marylanders, who, though unpaid, ill-clad and half-starved, performed their duties without a murmur, and from their ranks was no desertion. The militia were poorly armed, and dispirited by suffering from cold and hunger; while the enemy consisted of tried veterans, well-equipped, aggressive and enterprising, flushed with their success in Georgia and South Carolina, and led by one of the most skilful of the British captains.

These were the conditions under which Greene was to accomplish his arduous task; but he had a genius for the selection of his subordinates, and no General in the war was surrounded by a more brilliant group of officers. Smallwood, Williams and Howard, of Maryland: Sumner, Eaton and Davie, of North Carolina; Morgan, Lee, Washington, Pickens, Sumpter, Huger, Marion, Kirkwood, Carrington—what a list on the rolls of honour! And many a simple Lieutenant or Captain, as Duval of Maryland, and Forbis of North Carolina, is well worthy to be ranked with these illustrious leaders. Moreover, in this remarkable group of men—"all young, gallant, intelligent, and devoted to the cause"—there reigned great harmony, and we hear little of any jealousies or petty rivalries; so that of many of them might be said what Washington said of Greene himself: "Could he but promote the interests of his country in the character of a corporal, he would exchange without a murmur his epaulette for the knob." [1]

From Greene's letters we get a vivid picture of the situation and of his impressions. To Lafayette he wrote: "Were you to arrive, you would find a few ragged, half-starved troops in the wilderness, destitute of everything necessary for either the comfort or the convenience of soldiers." To Col. Coxe, on January 9th: "With an army without clothing or provisions, in a country exhausted, its currency ruined, the inhabitants divided, and our force less than a third of the enemy's, the prospect is dismal." And later to Sumpter, January 18th: "A number of my men have not a rag of clothes on them except a piece of blanket around their waists." [2] Moultrie's statement on this point is even stronger than Greene's; it is that the men "could scarcely cover their nakedness, and every little piece of cloth was taken up to tie about their waists."

On assuming command, Greene's first act was to appoint competent engineers to examine the fords and ferries of the great rivers, and he thus obtained information so accurate that Gen. Davidson said: "Greene had never seen the Catawba, yet he knew more about it than those who were raised on it." Cornwallis described North Carolina as "of all the Provinces in America the most difficult to attack,

[1] Garden's *Anecdotes*, 76.   [2] Johnson's *Greene*, I, 340, 341, 393.

on account of the numberless creeks and rivers, and the total want of internal navigation." [1] To be familiar with all the roads leading to the rivers, and with the means of crossing them, was absolutely indispensable, and the exact knowledge thus gained was the salvation of the army on its retreat.

Carrington was made Quartermaster-General, and Davie Commissary-General, two admirable appointments. Greene established the main army in a camp of repose and instruction at the falls of the Pee Dee river, 70 miles northeast of Cornwallis's camp at Winnsboro; and here he was joined, on January 12th, by "Light-Horse Harry Lee, the Eye of the Southern army," with his legion of picked men, 150 infantry and as many cavalry, for which Maryland furnished the horses.

To Morgan, who had been promoted General, a separate command was assigned, with orders to advance into South Carolina, to cross the Catawba, and operate on Cornwallis's left flank. His detachment consisted of about 1000 men, one-third of them North Carolinians and another third the veterans of the Maryland Line. Greene's instructions to Morgan were to employ this force against the enemy, either offensively or defensively, as his own prudence and discretion might direct. "The object of this detachment is to give protection to that part of the country and spirit up the people;

[1] Clinton-Cornwallis Controversy, I, 417.

to annoy the enemy in that quarter; to collect the provisions and forage out of their way. You will spare no pains to get good intelligence of the enemy's situation, and keep me constantly advised of both your and their movements."[1] On Christmas day Morgan took his post of observation on the Pacolet, one of the southern forks of Broad river, 50 miles northwest of Winnsboro, where he was joined by two hundred mounted militia of North and South Carolina.

IV.

1781. This was the situation of affairs at the close of the fateful year of 1780. Cornwallis was forced from his inactivity; for Greene on the Pee Dee and Morgan on the Pacolet threatened both his flanks. He resolved to attack them separately, and to renew the invasion of North Carolina, which he had abandoned after the defeat at King's Mountain. Supposing that Morgan was aiming at his stronghold of Ninety-Six, the British commander detached Tarleton with 1000 men to cover that post. To the order to "push Morgan to the utmost." Tarleton replied: "When I advance, I must either destroy Morgan's corps, or push it before me towards King's Mountain. I feel bold in offering my opinion. as it flows from well-

[1] Graham's *Morgan*, 260.

grounded inquiry concerning the enemy's designs and operations."[1]

As his main army lay between Greene and Morgan, Cornwallis, to make it uncertain which he would first strike, moved forty miles northwest from Winnsboro, between the Broad and Catawba rivers. Morgan retired to Hannah's Cowpens, four miles from the North Carolina line. This is in view of King's Mountain, and the sight of that hill of fame, still wet with patriots' blood, may have kindled in the breasts of Morgan's men a burning desire to meet with the edge of the sword an enemy as dangerous and as vindictive as Ferguson, for Tarleton's name had become a synonym for merciless cruelty.

On January 17th, Tarleton, after a fatiguing march of several hours, advanced to the attack, which Morgan awaited with his men rested, fresh, and eager for the fray. The American order of battle was the same as that adopted by Greene at Guilford, two lines of militia in front of the regulars. Both Generals have been criticised for this disposition of their troops, meeting with the weakest arm the first onrush of the enemy. But Morgan's purpose was to place his untried troops in a position which almost forced them to sell their lives dearly;[2] while Greene at Guilford felt con-

---

[1] Tarleton's *Campaigns*, 250, 252.   [2] Graham's *Morgan*, 316.

strained to hold his regulars in reserve; as he could in no wise risk the loss of the handful of veterans who formed the nucleus of the only army that could offer any resistance to the invasion.

The first line at Cowpens was composed of 150 North Carolina and Georgia riflemen, whose orders were to "mark the epaulette men," and to embarrass the enemy's advance by killing the officers; and then to retire behind the second line, which consisted of 300 militia of North and South Carolina under Gen. Pickens. The Spartan band of Marylanders, together with a small body of militia, formed the third line, stationed on a wooded hill; and behind them was Washington's cavalry in reserve.

Morgan was full of confidence, and in making his final rounds assured his men of coming triumph. "Give me two fires at killing distance," said he to the militia, "and I will make the victory sure."[1] His orders were strictly obeyed; as Tarleton advanced upon the riflemen, they retired behind the second line, firing, as they retreated, at "the epaulette men," with aim so deadly that the British line was thrown into confusion from loss of officers. Their brave and disciplined followers, however, continued to advance, and forced the militia of the second line to give way and reform in the rear of

[1] Greene's *Greene*, III, 144.

the Continentals.¹ Washington, meantime, had met and driven back the dragoons; but Tarleton, bringing up his reserves, hurled the full force of all his infantry upon the Marylanders. Firm as a rock they stood to receive the charge, until the movement of the militia on their right being misunderstood as a signal for retreat, they began slowly retiring. Alarmed by this, Morgan hurried up to Howard, who, pointing proudly to the firm ranks of his troops, that were marching as steadily as if on parade, asked: "Are men beaten who retreat in that order?"²

Lee's account of this turning point of the battle is that "the British line, considering the retrograde movement of the Marylanders the precursor of flight, rushed on with impetuosity; but, as it drew near, Howard faced about and gave it a close and murderous fire. Stunned by this unexpected shock, the enemy recoiled in confusion. Howard seized the happy moment, and followed up his advantage with the bayonet. This decisive step gave us the day. The weight of the battle fell upon Howard, who sustained himself admirably under trying circumstances, and seized with decision the

---

¹ Pickens ordered his militia to withhold their fire till it could be deadly; and when they were broken and retreating, rallied them, brought them again into action, and forced the enemy to surrender, which was never before effected with militia.—Garden's *Anecdotes*, 36.

² Graham's *Morgan*, 303.

critical moment to complete with the bayonet the advantage gained by his fire." [1]

The enemy, overwhelmed and helpless, threw down their arms, and fell upon their faces, begging for quarter: at one time it is said that Howard held in his hands the swords of seven British officers. "Give them Tarleton's quarters," was shouted along the American line by men eager to take vengeance for that leader's cruelties; but Howard's voice was as potent to restrain them from sullying their victory, as it had been to rouse them to deeds of daring. This is the supreme moment in that great soldier's brilliant career: the critical manœuvre of changing front in the height of the action was carried out with masterly skill and coolness, and he snatched victory from Tarleton's very grasp. Congress voted him a silver medal; and the title of "The hero of Cowpens" is the proudest that he bore. There is a tradition that his brilliant decisive movement was in disobedience of orders, and that Morgan's comment on it was: "You have done well, Col. Howard, for you have succeeded: had you failed, I should have had you shot."

Tarleton escaped with but a squadron of his dragoons, closely pursued by Col. Washington, and it is with this incident of the battle that is connected the well-known story of Tarleton saving

[1] Lee's *Memoirs*, 228, 230.

sneeringly to a North Carolina girl that he would like to see the famous American trooper, and receiving the withering reply:—" You could easily have seen him by looking back at Cowpens."

The much-needed war material which fell into the victor's hand comprised two cannon, 800 muskets, 100 horses and 35 waggons. The victory was as complete as that of King's Mountain: as there, the battle lasted but an hour, and it ended with the destruction of Cornwallis's best corps of light troops. The American loss was less than 80 killed and wounded; that of the British over 800, including prisoners, and very many officers. The riflemen had done their duty well: where they delivered their "two fires" the proportion of officers killed was very great, and "it was the magnanimous confession of a gallant officer of the Maryland Line, who fought on that day, that here the battle was gained."[1]

Morgan's masterly tactics at Cowpens make it the most brilliant battle of the war, and the chief factors in his success are the skill and coolness of the North Carolina riflemen,[2] and the courage and discipline of the Maryland Line. The losses here and at King's Mountain were a permanent and fatal weakening of Cornwallis's forces. He wrote

---

[1] Johnson's *Greene*, I, 380.
[2] " The militia behaved nobly; they did more than was required of them." Graham's *Morgan*, 300.

to Germain and Clinton:—"The unfortunate affair of January 17th was a very severe and unexpected blow; for besides reputation, our loss did not fall short of 600 men. It is impossible to foresee all the consequences that this extraordinary event may produce."[1]

Tarleton's account of his defeat, and his estimate of the importance of it, are of special interest. "When the Continentals gave ground, the British rushed forward. An order was despatched to the cavalry to charge; an unexpected fire from the Americans at this instant" (that was Howard's) "stopped the British, and threw them into confusion. Exertions to make them advance were useless, and an unaccountable panic extended itself along the whole line. All attempts to restore order or courage proved fruitless. . . . The fall of Ferguson at King's Mountain put a period to the first expedition into North Carolina; and the affair of the Cowpens overshadowed the commencement of the second."[1]

Sir Henry Clinton acknowledged that "the unfortunate day of Cowpens diminished Cornwallis's acting army nearly one-fourth; and those of his light troops which could least be spared in the move he was about to make."[2] And the British historian Stedman, the Commissary-General of

[1] Tarleton's *Campaigns*, 258, 267, 223, 227.
[2] Clinton-Cornwallis Controversy, 1, 102.

Cornwallis in this campaign, admits the supreme importance of Morgan's victory, by declaring that "the defeat of his majesty's troops at the Cowpens formed a very principal link in the chain of circumstances which led to the independence of America. Had Lord Cornwallis had with him at Guilford the troops lost by Col. Tarleton at the Cowpens, it is not extravagant to suppose that the American colonies might have been reunited to the empire of Great Britain."[1]

Seldom has a battle so momentous been fought with so small numbers; rarely has a victory so decisive been won at so slight a cost. Morgan's defeat would have meant the ruin of Greene's army, and the subjugation of North Carolina; his triumph was to lead to Guilford, Eutaw Springs and Yorktown. It is interesting now to note the truth of these prophetic words in the New Jersey *Gazette* of February 21st, when the news of Cowpens had just been received:—"This battle is but the prelude to the era of 1781, the close of which we hope will prove memorable in the annals of history, as the happy period of peace, liberty and independence to America."[2]

Ramsay tells us that "the glory and importance of the action at Cowpens resounded from one end of the Continent to the other. It re-animated the desponding friends of America, and seemed to be

[1] Stedman's *Hist.*, II, 325, 346.   [2] Moore's *Diary*, II, 375.

like a resurrection from the dead to the Southern States. Tarleton's repulse did more essential injury to the British interest than was compensated by all his victories."[1]

How natural that the patriots should hail this propitious opening of the campaign with joyful anticipations! The year 1780, with the surrender of Charleston, the disgrace of Camden, the treason of Arnold, had been a period of dire disaster; but King's Mountain had spanned its dying days with the bow of hope, and Cowpens gloriously ushered in the new year.

V.

As Cornwallis with the main army was but twenty-five miles from Cowpens, Morgan retreated northward immediately after the battle. The action was over at ten o'clock, and the march began by noon. His prisoners, guarded by a detachment of militia, were hurried forward into Virginia. Cornwallis followed, and on January 21st crossed the North Carolina line for the second invasion of the State. By forced marches, on January 23rd Morgan reached Sherrill's Ford of the Catawba, twenty-five miles from Ramsour's Mill, where Cornwallis arrived two days later.

Greene ordered his army to retire from the camp on the Pee Dee to Salisbury, and set out on Janu-

[1] Ramsay's *Hist. of S. C.*, I, 395, 396.

ary 28th, accompanied by only a sergeant's guard of cavalry, on a perilous march of 100 miles across the country to join Morgan. On the third day he came up with him on the Catawba, and, after a brief interview, rejoined his army at Salisbury.

Cornwallis reported to Clinton that "great exertions were made to intercept Morgan's corps on its retreat to the Catawba; but the celerity of their movements and the swelling of numberless creeks in our way rendered all our efforts fruitless. I therefore halted two days at Ramsour's Mill, collecting some flour, and destroying superfluous baggage and all my waggons, except those loaded with hospital stores, salt and ammunition."[1] An heroic measure to adopt, and one involving much sacrifice of comfort and convenience; but he thereby converted his whole army into a light corps capable of very rapid movement.

The retreat of Greene diagonally across the whole State of North Carolina, a distance of 230 miles from Cowpens to the river Dan in Virginia, is worthy to be ranked with the most famous retreats in the annals of war.[2] On no page of military history can be found greater skill of leadership, or more admirable examples of heroic endurance on

[1] Clinton-Cornwallis Controversy, I, 356.

[2] "The retreat of Gen. Greene and the pursuit of Lord Cornwallis, are worthy to be placed among the most remarkable events of the American war; they would have done honour to the most celebrated Captains of that, or any former epoch."—*Botta*, II, 319.

the part of the troops. Cornwallis was in hot pursuit with 4000 well-equipped veterans, while Greene could muster but 2000 men deprived almost of the necessaries of life. The roads were few and wretched; the country traversed by great rivers; the season cold and wet; and yet in this march of four weeks "in the very depth of winter, the men half-naked, marking their steps with blood which flowed from their bare feet; pinched with hunger, without tents, many destitute of blankets, drenched with perpetual rains, often wading waist deep through rapid streams—not one man deserted." [1]

Nor can praise for heroic endurance be denied to the enemy: both armies were exposed to the same hardships and suffering, though the British had the great advantage of being warmly clad. Greene wrote to Washington on February 15th:—" The miserable situation of the troops for want of clothing, has rendered the march the most painful imaginable; many hundreds of the soldiers tracking the ground with their bloody feet." [1]

None suffered more, or bore their trials more bravely, than the men of the Maryland Line. who were without tents from the time when they were assigned to Morgan's command till they crossed the Dan, a period of nearly two months. One of their Delaware fellow-soldiers wrote of them:—
" The manly fortitude of the Maryland Line was

[1] Johnson's *Greene*, I, 402, 435.

very great, being obliged to march barefoot, all the winter wanting coats and shoes, which they bore with the greatest patience imaginable, for which their praise should never be forgotten."[1] The figures are pathetically eloquent which tell us that at the end of the march the Maryland Line had but 861 men fit for duty, and 274, or nearly one-fourth their number, in the hospitals.

This, retreat was not only the admiration of the friends of the Revolution. it has called forth the most unqualified praises from every British writer.[2] While the story of it is the most painful, it is also the most inspiring page in the history of the campaign. Gallant deeds in the shock of battle stir the pulses and rouse the imagination to enthusiasm; but they are often surpassed in real courage and manliness by simple performance of duty under trying circumstances, by patient, heroic submission to every kind of suffering.

In all their trials the men were inspired and encouraged by the noble example of their great chief; there were none of their pains which he did not share, none of their burdens which he did not help to bear. At the post of duty at all hours of the night or day, after the battle of Guilford he wrote to his wife that he had not taken off his clothes for six weeks. As hopeful as he was brave, on but one occasion do we hear from him despondent

[1] Penn. *Hist. Magazine*, VII, 292.   [2] Johnson's *Greene*, I, 432.

words; and, familiar as is the story, it must be repeated here, for it commemorates the devotion of a noble woman. Gen. Greene arrived at Steele's tavern in Salisbury, after midnight, drenched with the rain and utterly exhausted. "Are you alone?" asked his host. "Yes, tired, hungry, alone and penniless." Mrs. Steele heard these words; she hastened to serve a hot supper to her guest, and then furtively drawing from under her apron two little bags of silver, said: "Take these, for you need them, and I can do without them."

Despondent he might well be, and doubtful as to the possibility of accomplishing results so great with means so inadequate; yet his letters at this time breathe a trust and confidence almost prophetic. On January 30th he wrote to Huger: "It is necessary we should take every possible precaution to guard against a misfortune. But I am not without hopes of ruining Lord Cornwallis, if he persists in his mad scheme of pushing through the country. Here is a fine field and great glory ahead." And again on February 5th: "From Cornwallis's pressing disposition and the contempt he has for our army, we may precipitate him into some capital misfortune."[1]

The British commanders gave full credit to Greene and his followers for their skill and courage in these trying days. Tarleton said, "Every meas-

[1] Johnson's *Greene*, I, 404, 424.

ure of the Americans, during their march from the Catawba to Virginia, was judiciously designed and vigorously executed."¹ Lord Germain wrote to Cornwallis, "The rebels conduct their enterprises in Carolina with more spirit and skill than they have shown in any other part of America."²

Greene divined all of his adversary's plans, and baffled them at every point. What those plans were is succinctly stated in Cornwallis's report of March 17th to Lord Germain:—"I hoped to destroy or drive out of South Carolina Gen. Morgan's corps; and I likewise hoped to get between Gen. Greene and Virginia, and force him to fight, without receiving reinforcements from that Province; or, failing of that, to oblige him to quit North Carolina with precipitation."²

In his pursuit of Morgan, Cornwallis reached Cowan's Ford of the Catawba on February 1st, where his crossing was bravely but vainly resisted by a body of North Carolina militia, who there lost their commander, Gen. Davidson, one of the best of Greene's officers. Beyond this point there was little further opposition on the march to the Yadkin. Tarleton reports that, learning that the militia were assembling at Torrance's tavern, he rode rapidly thither, and ordering his dragoons to "advance and remember the Cowpens," they

[1] Tarleton's *Campaigns*, 236.
[2] Clinton-Cornwallis Controversy, II, 10; and I, 355.

broke through the enemy killing and dispersing them.¹

After the fall of Davidson Gen. Pickens took command of the militia, about 700 in number, and followed in the trail of Cornwallis.

On February 3d Morgan crossed the Yadkin at Trading Ford, seven miles east of Salisbury, securing all the boats before the arrival of his pursuers; so that when Gen. O'Hara² with the advanced guard reached the opposite bank, he could only look regretfully at the deep waters and indulge in a vain cannonade. No loss was inflicted, but the incident is kept in memory by the fact that one of the balls shattered the roof of a cabin in which Greene was seated writing his reports; yet the General calmly "wrote on and seemed to note nothing but his despatches." Cornwallis's report is that "the guards came up with Morgan's rear at the Trading Ford of the Yadkin, which he had just passed. The river had now become impassable, and I determined to march to the upper fords—and with great expedition get between Greene and them —in hopes that he would not escape me without receiving a blow."³

---

[1] Tarleton's *Campaigns*, 232.

[2] It is not without interest to note that this is the same Gen. O'Hara who in 1793 was in command of the English garrison at Toulon, where he was wounded and taken prisoner in the famous attack upon the city which was the beginning of Napoleon's wonderful career.

[3] Clinton-Cornwallis Controversy, I, 359.

With this purpose he pushed forward, expecting to cut Greene off from the upper fords of the Dan, and force him to fight or surrender. But again was he foiled by the superior strategy of his wary adversary. Greene changed his course to Guilford Court House, where all the divisions of his army were reunited on February 8th, while the British were at Salem, but twenty-five miles distant. Here he reconnoitred the ground, and selected the field on which a month later he was to meet the enemy—Guilford, which Lord Germain said Cornwallis made forever "famous by the glorious victory gained there over the rebel forces;"[1] but the anniversary of which we celebrate as a seeming reverse which was to bring to us all the real fruits of a great triumph.

The day of decisive conflict however had not yet dawned; reinforcements were needed before an engagement could be risked, and the retreat was continued. On February 10th began the march to Irwin's Ferry, seventy miles from Guilford, where Greene intended to cross the Dan into Virginia. To protect his rear from the closely following enemy, he formed a special light corps of 700 men, composed of a detachment of the Maryland Line, of Lee's Legion and Washington's cavalry. The command was offered to Gen. Morgan, but ill health compelling him to retire from service, Col. Otho Williams was

[1] Clinton-Cornwallis Controversy, II, 10.

assigned to the post. The eminent services rendered by this select corps, both on the retreat and after the return of the army from Virginia to North Carolina, won the special thanks of the commanding general, and make one of the most brilliant pages in the annals of the Maryland Line.

We have noted Greene's wisdom in the choice of his Lieutenants, and nowhere did he show better judgment than in selecting Col. Williams to cover his retreat. Garden, one of Greene's aides-de-camp, who served under Williams in this campaign, credits him with possessing every requisite for the discharge of this difficult duty—coolness, endless resource, vigilance, military skill and prudence. He had elsewhere shown his great soldierly qualities, intrepidity on the battle field, discipline in camp, and intelligence in the cabinet; and now evincing "the most perfect self-command, he put nothing at hazard, and frequently suffered the opportunity to escape of acquiring advantages which would have increased his own fame, rather than risk what might, in its result, prove injurious to his country."[1]

The safety of the whole army depended upon this devoted band, and that this difficult retreat was successfully carried through, is largely due to Williams of Maryland. His task was to keep between Greene and Cornwallis, and to conceal

[1] Garden's *Anecdotes*, 59.

from the latter the movements of the American army. He therefore kept the British on his left and in his rear, and the Americans in front and on his right. In this critical position, with the pursuing enemy frequently in sight, ceaseless vigilance was indispensable, and the severest duty was exacted of the troops. Half of the men were alternately on night service as patrol, and none could have more than six hours rest in forty-eight. The daily march began long before dawn, to get far enough in advance of the enemy to allow time for cooking breakfast, the only regular meal of the day; and on reaching the halting-place at night, men and officers would fall upon the ground, too weary for food, craving only repose.

On February 14th the main army safely crossed the Dan at Irwin's Ford, and as soon as Williams learned this fact, he hastened after Greene with all speed, marching forty miles in one day; and Cornwallis reached the river the next morning only to see the enemy disappearing over the Virginia hills. The arduous task had been accomplished; "in the camp of Greene joy beamed in every face; and as if every man was conscious of having done his duty, the days subsequent to the reunion of the army on the north of the Dan were spent in mutual gratulations; with the rehearsal of the hopes and fears which agitated every breast during the retreat; interspersed with the many simple but interesting anecdotes with which every tongue was strung. No operation during the war attracted more the public attention, for the safety of the Southern Provinces hung upon its issue. Destroy Greene's army, and the Carolinas with Georgia inevitably became members of the British empire."[1]

Baffled and disappointed, Cornwallis relinquished the pursuit and turned aside to Hillsborough, to refresh his troops and to summon to his standard the Loyalists of North Carolina. The explanation of this movement, given in his report of March 17th to Lord Germain, is that "heavy rains and bad roads rendered all our exertions vain; for on our arrival at Boyd's ferry on February 15th, we found that Greene had crossed the day before. My force being ill-suited to enter by that quarter so powerful a province as Virginia, I proceeded to Hillsborough."[2]

The failure to destroy Greene's army must indeed have been a bitter disappointment; all the sacrifices, all the heroic efforts had been in vain. Tarleton however, in his account, makes light of the situation, and says: "The Continentals being chased out of North Carolina, and the militia awed, Earl Cornwallis thought the opportunity favorable for assembling the King's friends, and proceeded by easy marches to Hillsborough,"[3]

[1] Lee's *Memoirs*, 247, 251. [2] Clinton-Cornwallis Controversy, I, 360.
[3] Tarleton's *Campaigns*, 236.

where he opened correspondence with Major Craig, who had occupied Wilmington on January 29th. But he was soon to learn that the "King's friends" were far less numerous than was supposed; that the "chased Continentals" were deliberately returning to drive his lordship out of North Carolina; while the "awed militia" under Pickens presumptuously captured a picket post within a mile and a half of the British camp, on the very day of Cornwallis's arrival in Hillsborough.

It was plain there could be no repose for the troops, and within a week Cornwallis marched out again to the river Haw, and crossing it took post near Alamance Creek on February 27th; for the fleeing rebel had become the insolent aggressor; Greene had returned from Virginia, his army reinforced by Pickens's North Carolinians, and Campbell and Stevens's Virginia regulars and militia. Tarleton severely criticizes this movement of his chief, which was however forced upon him by Greene's strategy. "If Gen. Greene lost the confidence of his friends by quitting North Carolina, when pursued by a superior force, Earl Cornwallis likewise relinquished his claim to the superiority of the British arms by abandoning Hillsborough on the return of the American general into the Province." [1]

[1] Tarleton's *Campaigns*, 241.

VI.

The North Carolina Legislature at its session in January reduced the six battalions of Continentals to four, and devised means for raising a new force of regulars. Many volunteers having joined Greene, he at once resumed the offensive, and on February 23d recrossed the Dan, purposing to cut off Cornwallis from the upper country, and force him to retreat to Wilmington. Williams's flying corps had already been sent forward on February 18th; and he and Lee, together with Pickens's command, were keeping a close watch on the enemy's movements, and harassing him at every turn. An important skirmish took place at Whitsill's Mill on March 6th, where Williams's dash and energy were conspicuous. All of Cornwallis's manœuvres to destroy Greene's detachments in detail were baffled by the skill and caution of their commanders, and the various divisions of the American army finally forming a junction at High Rock, nothing remained for him but to try the fortune of a pitched battle.

This issue Greene was now willing to accept; for with augmented force he felt, if not confident of victory, at least hopeful of such a measure of success as would cripple his adversary. As he modestly expresses it in a letter to Jefferson five days before the battle of Guilford: " I trust I shall be able to proscribe the limits of the enemy's depredations, and at least dispose of the army in such a manner as to encumber him with a number of wounded men."¹

Determined now to risk an engagement, on March 14th Greene encamped on his chosen ground at Guilford Court-House. His army far outnumbered the enemy; but Cornwallis's troops were all veterans, while more than two-thirds of Greene's force consisted of new levies of militia. For them the field selected was very favourable, as it abounded in strong positions, and was in great part a forest, which afforded them protection against the push of the bayonet or the charge of cavalry. The only veterans were the 1st Maryland, Lee's Legion, and Washington's horse; though many of the officers of the recruits were tried soldiers.

Tarleton pronounces Guilford "one of the most hazardous, as well as severe battles of the war. The post occupied by Greene was extremely well chosen, and the manner of forming his troops unexceptionable."² The order of battle was that prudent disposition which we have noted at Cowpens, exposing the militia to the first onset of the

---

¹ Johnson's *Greene*, I, 474.

² Tarleton's *Campaigns*, 284.

Gen. O'Hara too said of Guilford: "No battle was ever more obstinately contested. Both armies were entitled to exalted praise." Garden's *Anecdotes*, 2nd Series, III, 173.

enemy, and reserving the regulars for a final defence, and to cover an orderly retreat. Greene's artillery consisted of but four six-pounders, and two of these, under Captain Singleton, were placed in the centre of the first line, commanding the road by which the British must approach. The van consisted of North Carolina recruits under Generals Eaton and Butler, stationed back of a clearing, with their flanks in the woods, protected by covering parties of riflemen and cavalry under Washington, Lee, and Campbell.

The Virginia militia composed the second line, 300 yards in the rear and entirely in the forest. Five hundred yards behind them was the third line of two brigades of Continentals; the one consisting of two Virginia regiments commanded by Gen. Huger, and the other of the First and Second Maryland under Williams, with Gunby and Ford as Colonels. Of these four regiments of regulars, the First Maryland, made up of the heroes of Camden and of Cowpens, is the only one that had been under fire. With this rear line were the remaining two cannon, and here was the General's post of observation during the action.

Cornwallis's camp was at the New Garden Quaker Meeting-House, between the forks of Deep River, twelve miles west of Guilford. At daybreak on the 15th he set out to find the rebel army. The morning was beautiful; the clear crisp atmosphere filled the soldiers' hearts with buoyant life and spirit, and braced their nerves to deeds of manly daring. Greene's army slept on the battle-field on the night of the 14th, and at early dawn Lee was sent out to reconnoitre. Meeting Tarleton's dragoons about four miles from Guilford, he engaged them in a sharp skirmish, and then retired to his post on the left wing of the Virginians.

It was high noon when Cornwallis came in sight of the American lines. On the British right was Bose's regiment and the 71st under Gen. Leslie, supported by a battalion of the Guards; on the left the 23rd and 33rd regiments commanded by Col. Webster, and supported by the Grenadiers and the 2nd battalion of the Guards under Gen. O'Hara. Under cover of an artillery fire, which was replied to by Singleton's two little guns, the British infantry advanced to the attack. Crossing the open field, they were received at fifty yards with so withering a fire from the North Carolinians, that Captain Stuart of the Scotch regiment declared that " one-half the Highlanders dropped on that spot." [1] and one of the riflemen said that " the part of the British line at which they aimed looked like the scattering stalks in a wheat field, when the harvest-man has passed over it with his cradle." [1] A moment later however, the British were upon them with the bayonet, turning their retreat into

[1] Caruthers' *Sketches of the Revolution*, 2d series, 134.

a disorderly flight; though Singleton saved his guns and withdrew with them to the left flank of the regulars.[1]

Dashing forward to the second line, the enemy met with a more obstinate resistance. Their right, under Leslie, became warmly engaged in front, flank and rear; while Webster's left being attacked in flank, he changed front to the left, supported by the Yagers and Guards. Scattering Lawson's Virginians, he advanced through the wood, and found himself face to face with the Continentals, who were drawn up on the brow of the opposite hill, a rough field traversed by a ravine intervening between them and the enemy.

Across this the British gallantly charged; but at the close distance of forty paces the 1st Maryland met them with a murderous fire before which they reeled and recoiled; and Gunby, dashing upon them with the bayonet, drove them back a broken mass across the ravine to the shelter of the woods. Many of their best fell here: Webster himself, Cornwallis's finest officer,[2] receiving a wound which

[1] For a full discussion of the conduct of the N. C. militia, see Schenck's *North Carolina*, 334–358.

[2] "To be first among the officers in the army under Lord Cornwallis, must be admitted to be no slight distinction; and this station had been long assigned with one voice to the gallant Webster. With this superiority in arms was combined the winning amiability which virtue in heart and virtue in habit never fail to produce, especially when united to the embellishment of literature and the manners of polished life."—Lee's *Memoirs*, 292.

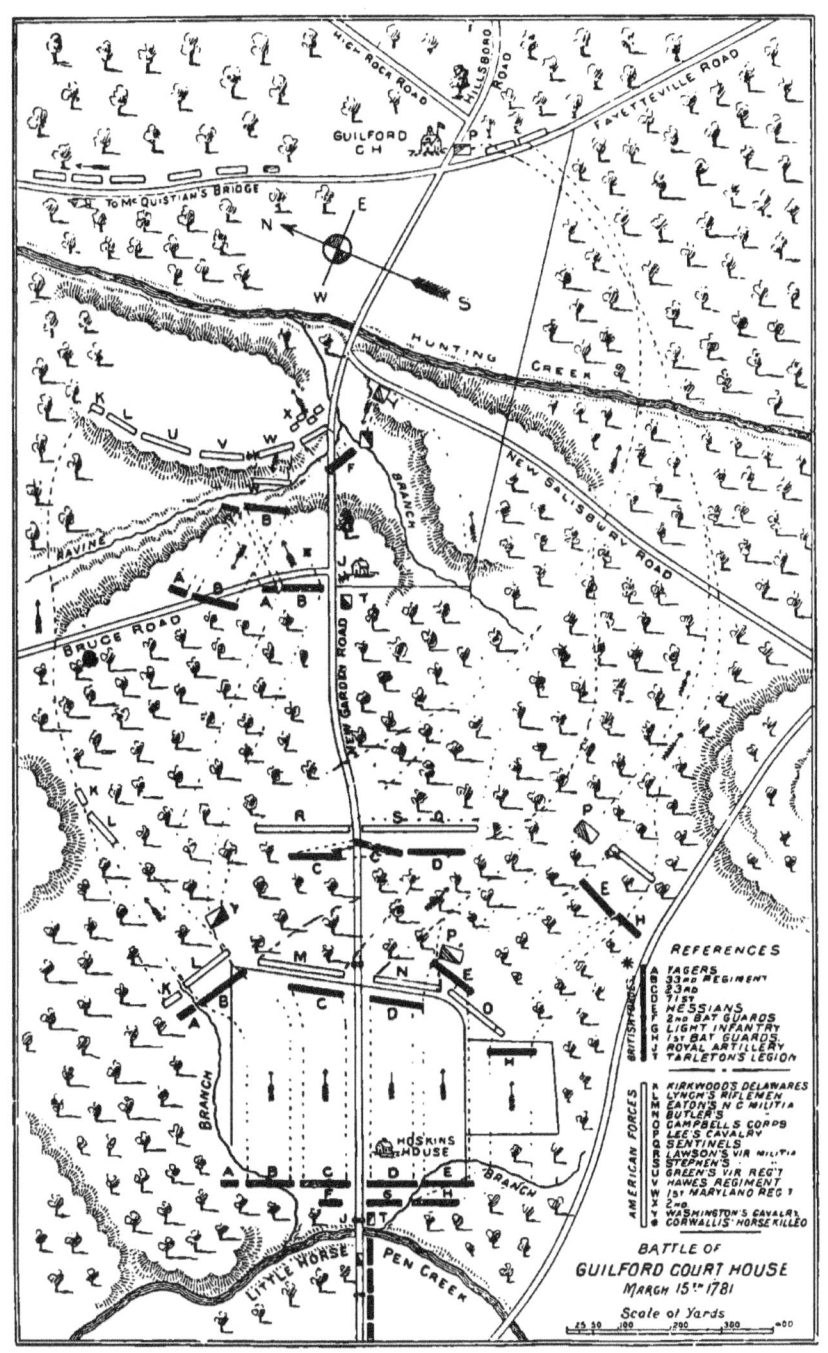

■ SITE OF THE MARYLAND MONUMENT.

proved mortal. As the 1st Maryland was returning to its position after this brilliant charge, Col. Stuart of the Guards fell upon the 2nd Maryland, which unhappily broke before the onset, and Singleton lost his guns.

Washington with his troop of horse was on a hill commanding Stuart's right, and from this point of vantage he bore down upon his flank, and burst through the ranks with a force irresistible. On the other flank came Howard—now in command, as Gunby had been unhorsed—with the terrible bayonets of the 1st Maryland, and a desperate fight ensued which was rarely paralleled during the war. The contest was hand to hand, and splendid were the examples of personal gallantry on both sides. Johnson tells the story of the tragic death of the British commander: "Two combatants particularly attracted the attention of those around them. These were Col. Stuart of the Guards and Captain John Smith of the Marylanders, both men conspicuous for nerve and sinew. They had met before (at Cowpens), and had vowed that their next meeting should end in blood. Regardless of the bayonets that were clashing around them, they rushed at each other with a fury that admitted of but one result. The quick pass of Stuart's small sword was skilfully put by with the left hand, whilst the heavy sabre of his antagonist cleft the Briton to the spine."[1]

[1] Johnson's *Greene*, II, 12.

Cornwallis seeing that the Guards were being cut to pieces, opened an artillery fire through his fleeing troops upon their pursuers, pouring volleys of grape on the mingled mass of friend and foe. The remedy was a desperate one, but there was none other left; he decimated a battalion of his best troops, but he stopped the advance of the resistless Marylanders. The British were now able to rally in full force, and Greene, unwilling to risk the destruction of his handful of Continentals, ordered a general retreat to Reedy Fork Creek, three miles in the rear. This movement was covered by the fresh regiment of Virginia regulars, which had not been in action, and after a halt here of some hours, the whole army retired to the Iron Works at Troublesome Creek, ten miles from Guilford. This retreat was conducted in a leisurely and orderly manner, unmolested by the enemy; for the victor was in no condition to follow up his advantage. A third of his men lay dead and wounded on the field, and among them were some of his best officers. Cornwallis's report says "Our troops were excessively fatigued by the action, which had lasted an hour and a half, and our numerous wounded demanded immediate attention, so that we could not pursue."[1]

Both Generals had exposed themselves recklessly: Cornwallis had two horses killed under

[1] Clinton-Cornwallis Controversy, I, 367.

him, and Greene narrowly escaped capture. The fight was brief, but at the end of it the American General fainted from exhaustion.

We are told that while the battle was raging, all the women of the neighbourhood were at prayer. What a touching and dramatic scene does this suggest! The air is filled with the sounds of strife,— the roar of cannon, the heavy tread of man and horse, the exultant shout, the groans of agony and despair,—and amidst it all rise to the eternal throne the pathetic petitions :—

" Have mercy upon me, O God, and give me the comfort of Thy help !

" Fight Thou, O Lord, against them that fight against me.

" It is not my sword that shall help me ; but it is Thou that savest us.

"Stand up, O Lord God of Hosts, and deliver us from our enemies ! "

The night that followed the battle was one of horror : it was impossible to minister to the many wounded of both armies : a cold rain added to their suffering, and many died before morning from loss of blood, from cold and exposure.

The long-sought battle was fought and won ; Cornwallis had at last tasted the fruit of victory, but only to find that it turned to ashes on his lips. " The brilliant victory of March 15th," wrote Sir Henry Clinton, " had all the consequences of defeat." "Another such victory," exclaimed Fox in Parliament. "will ruin the British army! From the report of Cornwallis there is the most conclusive evidence that the war is at once impracticable in its object and ruinous in its progress."[1]

Though tactically a defeat for the Americans, Guilford was strategically a decisive victory, and the most important one since the capture of Burgoyne.[2] Tarleton's statement is that "the ability of the English commander, seconded by the vigour and resolution of his officers and soldiers, with extreme difficulty forced the enemy from their position, and in that fortunate exploit the British army was crippled, by the quality and number of the officers and men killed and wounded. The victory, however honourable to the General and the troops, was not useful or advantageous to Great Britain."[3]

Cornwallis had made every possible effort to insure complete success, and his men had bravely responded to all his demands upon them. While the American soldiers won imperishable renown at Guilford, it is equally true that no battle of the war reflects more honour on the courage of the British troops; for on no other occasion did they fight with such inferiority of numbers, or disadvantages of ground.[4] Lee declared that "on no

[1] Bancroft, V, 495.
[2] Fiske's *Amer. Rev.*, II, 260.
[3] Tarleton's *Campaigns*, 285, 286.
[4] Marshall's *Washington*, IV, 371.

occasion, in any part of the world, was British valour more heroically displayed."¹

Of the American officers who died on the field none was a greater loss to his country than Major Anderson of the 1st Maryland. He had done splendid service at Camden, and now shared in all the glory won by his regiment at Guilford; it is most fitting that his honoured dust should mingle with this historic soil. The conduct of the 1st Maryland has received most lavish praise from all quarters. Johnson challenges " the modern world to produce an instance of better service performed by the same number of men in the same time."² They routed the famous 33d regiment, and drove its shattered ranks into the forest; then breaking through the flank of the Guards, who, on account of the dense woods, had passed their left unseen, they, with Washington's cavalry, scattered like chaff the flower of the British army. Checked in the pursuit by the enemy's artillery, they returned to their position in perfect order. Proud may Maryland be of such an example of courage and discipline! Washington wrote to Greene on April 18th: " I am truly sensible of the merits and fortitude of the veteran bands under your command, and wish the sentiments I entertain of their worth could be communicated with the warmth I feel."²

¹ Lee's *Memoirs*, 286.   ² Johnson's *Greene*, II, 15, 25.

Greene could not know that Guilford was the decisive event of the campaign, or that its result would be the abandonment of North Carolina by Lord Cornwallis, and his ultimate surrender at Yorktown; but he knew that he had dealt a mortal blow to British power in the South. In an interesting letter to Reed, written but three days after the fight, he says:—"The battle was long, obstinate and bloody. We were obliged to give up the ground, and lost our artillery; but the enemy have been so soundly beaten, that they dare not move towards us since the action, notwithstanding we lay within ten miles of them for two days. Except the ground and the artillery, they have gained no advantage: on the contrary they are little short of being ruined. We have little to eat, less to drink, and lodge in the woods in the midst of smoke. Never did an army labour under so many disadvantages as this; but the fortitude and patience of the officers and soldiery rise superior to all difficulties. I have never felt an easy moment since the enemy crossed the Catawba until since the defeat of the 15th, but now I am perfectly easy, being persuaded it is out of the enemy's power to do us any great injury."[1]

The temporary check led to a permanent success, and the biographer of Burke cites Guilford as a "type in this respect of the whole American war;

[1] Reed's *Reed*, II. 350.

a battle won was scarcely more advantageous than a battle lost, and to conquer was not to subdue. This signal victory was attended with all the consequences of a defeat."[1]

The battle of King's Mountain drove Cornwallis back into South Carolina; the defeat at the Cowpens made his second invasion of North Carolina a desperate enterprise; the battle at Guilford Court-House transformed the American army into pursuers, the British into fugitives.[2]

VII.

From the battle-field Cornwallis retired to his camp at the New Garden Meeting House, and on March 18th, he issued a proclamation[3] thanking God

[1] McKnight, *Life of Burke*, II, 435.
[2] Bancroft's *U. S.*, old edition, X, 479.
[3] A parody on Cornwallis's proclamation was written in camp on March 30th, 1781, by St. George Tucker, of Virginia.

"Whereas by providence divine
Which on our arms has deigned to shine,
On Thursday last we fought a battle
With lousy, vile rebellious cattle,
And to our everlasting glory
(Unaided by a single Tory)
The rebel forces did defeat,
And gain a victory compleat:
I therefore, willing to uphold
The weak, and to reward the bold,
Do issue this my Proclamation,
Without regard to sect or station,

for his "signal success and complete victory over the rebel forces," and calling on all Loyalists to "stand forth and take an active part in restoring good order and government;" yet on that very day he destroyed his baggage, left behind his hospital with seventy-five wounded men, and began a hasty retreat to the sea-coast. He had tried to bribe his prisoners to renounce their allegiance to the American cause, assuring them that it was utterly lost, and that Greene was hopelessly ruined. While an English officer was thus tempting the men to desert their colours, "the sound of the morning guns from Greene's camp came reverberating from the hills. An old Tar Heel heard the familiar signal, and cried out: 'Listen, Boys! the old cock is crowing again,' and a shout of defiance went up that convinced the English officer that patriotism in the old North State was above

>Requiring every loyal Tory
>To come to me and share the glory
>And toil of bringing back to reason
>The wretches guilty of high treason.
>Whereby the government benign
>Of Britain's majesty divine
>With lustre primitive may shine.
>
>Let no ill-natured imputation
>Be cast on this our Proclamation,
>Because from hence, with God's permission,
>I mean to march with expedition:
>Though I confess we do not mean
>To go in quest of Mr. Greene." etc.
>
>*Mag. of Amer. Hist.*, VII, 45.

the temptation of bribery or the intimidation of British power."[1]

Forced to retire to the coast, Cornwallis crossed the Deep River at Ramsay's Mill, and marched down the right bank of the Cape Fear to Wilmington, where he arrived on April 7th. Greene followed for a while his retreating rival, and on March 21st he wrote to Lee, who had been sent forward on a reconnaissance, "Forward me the best intelligence you can get: I mean to fight the enemy again: Lord Cornwallis must be soundly beaten before he will relinquish his hold."[2] He evidently then expected to overtake his fleeing adversary, and strike him on the march; but he soon changed his plan, and resolved to accomplish indirectly his purpose of relieving North Carolina of the presence of the enemy.

On March 29th he wrote to Washington: "I am determined to carry the war immediately into South Carolina. The enemy will be obliged to follow us or give up his posts in that State. If the former takes place, it will draw the war out of this State and give it an opportunity to raise its proportion of men. If they leave their posts to fall, they must lose more than they can gain here."[3] Lord Rawdon, one of Cornwallis's able Lieutenants, who was then in command in South Carolina, had

[1] Schenck's *North Carolina*, 372. [2] Lee's *Memoirs*, 288.
[3] Johnson's *Greene*, II. 37.

a long line of defences extending from Charleston by way of Camden and Ninety-Six to Augusta, Georgia, and Greene might strike this at any point.

Accordingly, after gathering supplies and giving his troops some days of rest, on April 6th he crossed Deep River at Ramsay's Mill and marched westward to the Yadkin, whence by easy stages he reached Hobkirk's Hill near Camden on April 20th. This post of evil memory was under the command of Rawdon in person, and he, kept informed by Tories of all Greene's movements, was able to surprise him by a sudden attack on the morning of the 25th.

The Americans were posted on a ridge with their flanks covered by a forest and a swamp, and the line of battle was quickly formed with the Maryland and Virginia brigades of Continentals in front, and Washington's cavalry with Col. Read's North Carolina militia in the rear. The British attack was sharp, but it was firmly met by the regulars, who were ordered to charge with fixed bayonets down the hill on the advancing foe, while Ford, of the 2nd Maryland, and Washington were to strike him in flank and rear. From the success of this movement Greene promised himself a complete victory; but it failed because the regiment on which he chiefly depended, the 1st Maryland, made up of the heroes of many battles, was thrown into disorder and gave way before the enemy.

They were rallied by Gunby and Howard, but it was then too late. Lee's account is that "in this movement the veteran regiment of Gunby, having first joined in the fire, in violation of orders, paused; its right falling back. Gunby unfortunately directed the disordered battalion to rally by retiring to its right company. Retrograde being the consequence of this order, the British line, giving a shout, pressed forward with redoubled ardour; and the regiment of Gunby, considered as the bulwark of the army, never recovered from the panic with which it was at this moment unaccountably seized."[1]

The 2nd Maryland behaved with great gallantry, and fully retrieved the reputation it had lost at Guilford; but its valiant leader Ford being mortally wounded, it began to yield, and Greene to save his army ordered a general retreat.

The action at Hobkirk's was a decided reverse for the American arms, though Rawdon was unable to profit by his victory. The losses were equal, about one-fourth of the number engaged; but on our side they included such valuable officers as Lieut.-Col. Ford and Captain Beatty of Maryland, whom Greene eulogizes in his report of the battle as " one of the best of officers, and an ornament to his profession." It was not a day of glory for our troops, and Greene ascribed the disaster entirely to the error of Col. Gunby; yet the " hero of Hob-

[1] Lee's *Memoirs*, 337.

kirk," as the "hero of Cowpens," was a Marylander. Captain John Smith, whose desperate fight with Col. Stuart we have noticed at Guilford, was ordered with forty-five picked men to rescue three pieces of artillery which were exposed to capture by the enemy. The danger was so imminent that Greene himself dismounted and seized the ropes to drag off the guns. The British cavalry charged again and again to secure the prize, but were repulsed by the little band of Marylanders: until Rawdon's infantry joining in the attack, every man of Smith's company was killed or captured.

Some weeks later, when he had recovered from his wounds, Smith was released on parole and set out on foot for Charleston. On the road he was seized by a party of British soldiers, stripped and cruelly beaten. At Charleston he became intimate with some English officers, and meeting one day at their quarters an officer who had taken part in this deed of shame, he expressed to his friends surprise that they would associate with a man capable of an act of dishonour. Asked to explain, he told the story of his disgrace and suffering. "Then kick him, Smith," was the general reply, "and he had the gratification of kicking the rascal out of the company." [1]

Col. Gunby, pained by the criticisms on his conduct in the field, demanded a court-martial, which

[1] Johnson's *Traditions of the Revolution*, 365.

was granted him. Its finding was that "Gunby's spirit and activity were unexceptionable; but his order for the regiment to retire was improper and unmilitary, and in all probability the only cause why we did not obtain a complete victory." He soon after retired from service, stung to the heart by this unhappy close of his brilliant career. A striking instance of the caprice of fortune! Gunby attempted at Hobkirk's Hill the same movement that Howard accomplished so successfully at Cowpens; to the one it brought ruin, to the other undying fame.

The defeat at Hobkirk's did not change the plans of the American commander, or bring any permanent advantage to the victor. Greene continued to threaten the British stronghold at Camden, and a fortnight after the battle Lord Rawdon abandoned the post, after burning all his stores and the public buildings. Greene's repulse at Guilford had freed all western North Carolina; his defeat at Hobkirk's was speedily followed by the recovery of Camden. Despite apparent failure, his strategic movement into South Carolina was already successful in its aim. Tarleton acknowledges that "the wisdom and vigour of the American operations deranged all the designs of Earl Cornwallis at Wilmington."[1] On April 23rd, there-

[1] Tarleton's *Campaigns*, 290.

fore on the eve of the affair at Hobkirk's, the Earl wrote to Lord Germain that it was impossible for him to return to Camden, to aid Lord Rawdon and save South Carolina, for any disaster to his army would make general a spirit of revolt in that Province,—that Greene might hem him in among the great rivers and cut off his subsistence,—therefore he would take advantage of Greene's leaving lower Virginia open, and march immediately into that Province, and join Gen. Phillips at Petersburg.[1] These are very significant words: not six weeks have elapsed since the "glorious victory" at Guilford, and already we see foreshadowed the abandonment of all his conquests in the Carolinas, and the fateful march to Yorktown.

After Hobkirk's the minor British posts fell in rapid succession: Fort Watson had surrendered on April 23, Camden was abandoned on May 10, Orangeburg May 11, Fort Motte May 12, Nelson's Ferry May 14, Fort Granby May 15, and Georgetown,—all within three weeks. Apart from the seaports, which were protected by the British fleet, at the end of May there remained but two important posts in the enemy's power, Augusta and Ninety-Six. The former surrendered to Gen. Pickens on June 5th, when the gallant Major Eaton fell, and all Georgia except Savannah was redeemed from British rule.

[1] Clinton-Cornwallis Controversy, I, 421.

Greene now concentrated his forces for the siege of Ninety-Six, which he had invested on May 26th; and Lord Rawdon, who had been reinforced by three regiments of fresh troops, hastened to its relief. Informed of his approach, Greene attempted to carry the fort by storm, and met with a bloody repulse, his loss being more than double that of the enemy. In this assault Lieutenants Duval of Maryland and Selden of Virginia led the forlorn hope. They leaped into the ditch, and began tearing down the abatis; but they were received with a terrible cross-fire, and the height of the parapet foiled all their heroic efforts. Very few of their men were unhurt, and the ditch was filled with the wounded and dead. The sacrifice was in vain, but again had Maryland cause to be proud of the gallantry of her young heroes. "Never was greater bravery exhibited than by the parties led on by Duval and Selden. Both these officers were wounded, and the greater part of their men wounded or killed."[1] Equal heroism was displayed by the enemy; and it is worthy of note that the valiant defenders of Ninety-Six,—as afterwards of the brick house at Eutaw Springs,—were Americans, a resolute band of Provincials led by Lieut. Col. Cruger of New York.

Greene abandoned the siege and retreated rapidly northward; Rawdon, now far superior in

[1] Greene's Report, Tarleton, 514.

numbers, trying in vain to overtake him and force him to fight. Failing in this, the British General determined to evacuate Ninety-Six, and to withdraw to a line of defence nearer the sea; the Santee, Congaree and Edisto rivers now becoming the limits of British sway. The greater part of South Carolina had thus in a short time been recovered, though the patriots had won no battle. As the hot and sickly season came on, Greene took post on July 16th in the healthful region of the hill country on the Santee, and gave his exhausted soldiers a brief repose.[1]

VIII.

In the meantime, under the greatest and most discouraging difficulties, Gen. Jethro Sumner[2] had raised and equipped a new brigade of North Carolina Continentals, to replace those surrendered by Lincoln at Charleston. With this addition to his army Greene would be compensated for the reinforcements which Rawdon had received, and could

---

[1] Washington wrote Greene on July 30th: "I am unable to conceive what more could have been done under your circumstances, than has been displayed by your little persevering and determined army."—Ford's *Washington*, IX, 319.

[2] Generals Jethro Sumner and Robert Howe, Colonels Thomas Clarke and Hardy Murfree, Majors Reading Blount and William Polk, Captains John Daves and Edward Yarborough, Lieutenants Thomas Pasteur and Richard Fenner, with fifty other officers of the Continental Line, were the original members of the North Carolina Society of the Cincinnati.

once more take the field. The difficulty of procuring arms and clothing for these troops was so great that not until July were they ready to enter upon the campaign; and but for their good fortune in getting some muskets from Virginia, the North Carolinians might not have been in time to share the glories of Eutaw. The hardships which the men had to endure were no less than in the Guilford campaign, except that they were not exposed to the cold and rains of winter. Major John Armstrong wrote to Gen. Sumner on July 1st from the camp between the Broad and Catawba rivers: "We are without money, clothing, or any kind of nourishment for our sick; not one gill of rum, sugar or coffee; no tents or camp kettles or canteens; no doctor, no medicine." There is a touch of pathos in the words "We are in a fine situation; plenty of good water. It hath one failing—it will not *make grog.*"[1]

By August 15th all difficulties had been overcome, and Sumner joined Greene with 800 regulars, in addition to the North Carolina militia already in camp. The American General now felt strong enough again to meet the enemy in the open field and try the issue of battle. The greatest heats of summer were past, the troops were rested and thoroughly drilled, and he might hope by one decisive blow to overthrow forever the British

[1] Schenck's *North Carolina*, 434.

power in the South. Accordingly he broke up camp on August 23d, and marched towards the enemy, who was at no great distance on the other side of the Santee river.

Lord Rawdon had sailed for England, and Col. Stewart, now in command of the British forces, retired towards his defences at Charleston, and halted at the springs where Eutaw Creek empties into the Santee, in an admirable position, which he thought his adversary would not venture to attack. His right flank was perfectly protected by the Creek, and on its banks was a clearing, in which was a palisaded garden and a brick house, that might serve as a fortress of refuge in case of disaster. The woods covered the left flank, and the Springs the approaches from the rear; while from the centre of the camp radiated two roads which formed safe avenues of retreat.

The approach of Greene was unknown to the enemy, and early in the morning of September 8th his advanced guard surprised and captured the British "rooting party," as the foragers for sweet potatoes were called. The day was clear and calm, and it was growing warm as the two armies came in sight of each other and formed in order of battle. The British were drawn up in a single line, Major Coffin's cavalry covering their left, while the corps of Major Majoribanks, a brave and skilful officer, was posted in the woods on the right.

Greene's order of battle was the same as at Guilford, the militia in front and the regulars in the rear. The militia of North Carolina and South Carolina under Malmedy, Pickens and Marion formed the first line, with their flanks covered by Lee's Legion and Henderson's volunteers, many of whom were North Carolinians. The second line was composed of the Continentals; the Virginians under Col. Campbell in the centre; the Marylanders and North Carolinians on the left and right under Williams and Sumner. Washington's cavalry was in reserve.

The enemy attacked with their wonted impetuosity, but the brave Carolinians stood firm against the onset of the whole British army. In no battle of the war did the militia perform more brilliant service: it seemed as though in this last great fight for liberty they must make amends for all former failures, and show that any want of steadiness under fire was due merely to lack of opportunity for drill and discipline.[1] Greene himself, though his mind was filled with the trained soldier's distrust of irregular levies, wrote to Baron von Steuben that "such conduct would have graced the veterans of the great king of Prussia."[2] And Johnson said that "it was

---

Many of these soldiers were the same that were accused of abandoning the field at Guilford, and they now behaved with such gallantry that of 300 in action 190 were killed or wounded. Garden's *Anecdotes*, 40.

[2] Johnson's *Greene*, II, 225.

with equal astonishment that both the American regulars and the troops of the enemy contemplated these men, steadily and without faltering, advance with shouts into the hottest of the enemy's fire, unaffected by the continual fall of their comrades around them."[1] They were greatly outnumbered, and they were facing the king's best regiments, but they did not yield till they had fired seventeen rounds, and their artillery was disabled.

When the militia retreated, Sumner promptly moved forward his three battalions of North Carolina Continentals, under Ashe, Blount and Armstrong, and reformed the line of battle. This brigade was composed of the new levies that had been under military drill but little more than a month; yet they were as cool and steady as veterans, and exhibited admirable courage and discipline. Greene reported that "the North Carolina brigade under Sumner, though not above three months raised, behaved nobly. I am at a loss which most to admire, the gallantry of the officers or the good conduct of their men."[2]

The British line was broken by the Carolinians, and now came the turn of the Marylanders in this dance of death. "Let Williams advance and sweep the field with his bayonets," was the order from Greene. Like a whirlwind came these heroes,

[1] Johnson's *Greene*, II, 225.
[2] Tarleton's *Campaigns*, 530. Johnson's *Greene*, II, 225.

and nothing could withstand their desperate onset.
Stewart brought up his last reserves, but all were
swept away before this resistless tide of steel. The
enemy performed prodigies of valour, and many of
the Irish Buffs and of the Marylanders fell face to
face, transfixed with each other's bayonets. The
veteran leaders who had witnessed many a brave
struggle, were thrilled with admiration for the
heroism here displayed. Otho Williams wrote:
" To have an idea of the vivacity and intrepidity of
the American troops, you must have shared their
danger and seen their charge, which exceeded anything of the sort I ever saw before."[1] And Gen.
Greene: " Nothing could exceed the gallantry of
the Maryland Line. Col. Williams's uncommon
intrepidity in leading on the Maryland troops to
the charge, surpasses anything I ever saw. I cannot forbear praising the conduct and courage of
all my troops. Never did men or officers offer
their blood more willingly in the service of their
country."[2]

A signal victory seemed absolutely certain; but
again fickle fortune changed. The fleeing enemy
entrenched themselves in the brick house and
palisaded garden, and Major Majoribanks gallantly
held his position on the right. On the American
side the loss of officers had been very great; few

[1] Tiffany's *Memoir of Williams*, 25. [2] Moore's *Diary*, II, 490.

of the commanders of regiments were unhurt.
Only a Lieutenant remained to command Washington's troop, and Henderson, Howard, Campbell,
with other brilliant officers were wounded. The
men broke ranks and began plundering the enemy's
camp. Poor fellows! few of the good things of
life fell to their lot, and British fare and British
rum were not to be resisted.

In this confusion Stewart returned vigorously
to the attack, captured Greene's artillery, and
forced him to order a retreat. Greene rallied his
men on the ground where the action began, and
both sides were too much exhausted to renew the
fight. Each could claim the victory,[1] though as
usual all the fruits of it fell to the Americans.
Greene retired some miles, and then turning began
a pursuit of the enemy, who after destroying their
stores and a thousand stand of arms, abandoned
many of the wounded, and retreated to their seacoast defences.

For the numbers engaged few battles have been
bloodier, and victory was bought at a terrible
sacrifice. The American loss was about 500
killed and wounded; that of the British as great,

---

[1] "There were at Eutaw two successive engagements. In the first Greene won brilliantly and with little loss; in the second he sustained a defeat, with the death or capture of many of his bravest men. '*C'est une grande chose de savoir s'arrêter à temps,*' wrote to Lafayette Count de Vergennes, Minister of Foreign Affairs in France, commenting on the incidents of this battle." Bancroft, old edition, X, 494.

besides several hundred prisoners. Twenty-one of Greene's officers died on the field, among them Lieut. Duval the Maryland hero of Ninety-Six.[1] Greene complimented his men on the field; Congress passed a flattering vote of thanks to the troops, and presented to the General a British standard and a gold medal emblematical of the battle and victory.

To General Greene is due indeed an unstinted meed of praise: few commanders have had greater difficulties to encounter; none with the same means have accomplished more. He had been in command less than ten months; he had won no decisive victory, and had been favoured by no brilliant stroke of fortune; yet the three Southern Provinces were completely freed from the presence of the enemy, with the exception of the seaports of Wilmington, Charleston and Savannah. "The Southern States," wrote Otho Williams after Eutaw, "were lost, they are now restored: the American arms were in disgrace; they are now in high reputation."[2] For the men who wrought this happy change no reward and no encomium can be too great. Nor can we forget the merit of their adversaries; men not of a different race, but of the same

---

[1] "The service did not boast an officer of more consummate valour, or higher promise, than Lieut. Duval. At Ninety-Six he led the forlorn hope, and at Eutaw he had captured a field-piece, when he was killed." Garden's *Anecdotes*, 95.

[2] Tiffany's *Memoir of Williams*, 28.

blood, and endowed with the same qualities as our heroes. What soldiers they were is shown by the fact that Eutaw is among the very few instances during the war where the British army was driven from its ground in a pitched battle. Tarleton said truly: "It is impossible to do justice to the spirit, patience, and invincible fortitude displayed by the British officers and soldiers during these dreadful campaigns in the two Carolinas. They displayed military and moral virtues far above all praise. Justice too requires that the Americans should not be deprived of their share of this fatal glory. They had the same difficulties to encounter, joined to a fortune in the field generally adverse."[1]

After Eutaw Greene returned to his hill-camp to recruit the army; but the war was practically over, and the country had little further need of the services of these heroes. Their exploits had been as brilliant as any that adorn the pages of history, and their manly endurance of every kind of hardship is beyond all praise. Great trials were borne not merely with resignation, but with that marvellous buoyancy of spirits which was again so characteristic of the Confederate soldier: they made light of all their pains, and their distress was provocative of infinite wit. "The soldiers were merry with their misfortunes. They used 'starvation' as a cant-word, and vied with each other in

[1] Tarleton's *Campaigns*, 523.

burlesquing their situation. The wit and humour displayed contributed not a little to reconcile them to their sufferings."[1]

The genius of Greene, the valour and skill of his officers, and the splendid conduct of the Southern troops, had brought the war to a happy close, and won independence for America. The British power in the Colonies was utterly broken, and a month later the surrender at Yorktown formed the last scene in the sanguinary drama.

IX.

The battle of Eutaw is a most fitting conclusion to this imperfect sketch of the exploits of the sons of Maryland and of North Carolina; a field on which more than half of the dead and wounded were North Carolinians, and where the men of the Maryland Line ended so brilliantly their five years of illustrious service. But it is on the battle-ground of Guilford that these achievements are most appropriately commemorated; for both in point of time and of importance Guilford is the central incident in the stirring twelvemonth between Camden and Eutaw; up to it all previous events naturally lead, and from it all subsequent ones logically flow.

It is to commemorate the deeds that we have described, to keep alive the memory of heroes such

[1] Ramsay's *Hist. of the Rev.*, II, 164.

as these, that this monument is erected. It is a
simple block of Maryland granite, and on it are
inscribed no names; for where all did so well,
there should be no invidious distinction between
officer and private. The same "meed of some
melodious tear" is due to the noble Anderson,
whose body has here mouldered into dust, as to
the humblest soldier over whose nameless grave
we place this memorial stone.

A recent historian has said that Maryland "has
strangely forgotten the memory of those who gave
this nation an existence. No mark distinguishes
the resting-place of Major Anderson, a reproach
which ought not longer to rest on his fellow-
citizens, who followed after to enjoy the blessings
purchased with his blood."[1] That reproach is now
wiped out, and we have inscribed in bronze that
this is "Maryland's tribute to her heroic dead;"
adding merely the words "non omnis moriar."
How true, how prophetic they are! The name of
the poet who first uttered those proud words is as
familiar to us to-day as it was to his contemporaries
of the Augustan age. The truly great cannot
wholly die, for their deeds live after them, and the
good which they have wrought remains the permanent inheritance of mankind.

The battle-field is the last resting-place of our
honoured dead, but we remember with Perikles that

[1] Schenck's *North Carolina*, 222, 223.

"the whole earth is the sepulchre of illustrious men; and not only are they commemorated by columns and inscriptions in their own country, but in lands not their own there dwells also an unwritten memorial of them, graven not on stone, but in the hearts of men."[1]

The only ornament of this rugged granite block is the beautiful coat-of-arms which Maryland adopted from the armorial bearings of the Lords Baltimore. Its significant motto "Fatti maschi, Parole femine."—Manly deeds, Womanly words,—suggests the ideal of the knightly character, of the true gentleman; thoroughly brave and masculine, yet gentle and tender as a woman. We proudly believe that it describes the true Marylander, and it may serve as a fitting epitaph for the men who made this spot famous.

The ceremonies of dedication of this monument have vividly recalled the early historic connection between the commonwealths of Maryland and North Carolina; and there has never since been a time when antagonism of interest has placed them in an attitude of hostility. With the same hopes and the same memories, they must always remain united in closest friendship.

"Nam idem velle atque idem nolle, ea demum firma amicitia est."[2]

[1] Thoukydides, II, 43.
[2] Sallust, *Cat.*, 20, 4.

To the care of the Guilford Battle-Ground Company we have confided the ashes of our valiant dead, and placing this Maryland monument on Carolina soil, we add another link to the golden chain of sentiment which binds together the sister States.

"The silence of a hundred years upon these graves has lain;
 Where sleep our noble heroes, in freedom's battle slain.
 The springtime in its beauty, the summer in its prime,
 The dropping leaves of autumn, each gladsome Christmas chime,
 Alike have passed unnoted by the quiet slumberers here:
 They lie in glory,—let them rest, knowing no pain nor fear.
 'Tis ours to rear a granite shaft, 'neath heaven's o'er-arching dome,
 And link each name with deathless fame for all the years to come."

www.ingramcontent.com/pod-product-compliance
Lightning Source LLC
Chambersburg PA
CBHW020148170426
43199CB00010B/934